THE EXECUTION OF MARY ANSELL

MOLLY WHITTINGTON-EGAN

THE EXECUTION OF MARY ANSELL

First edition published 2017 (Hardcover)
This Edition 2019 (Softcover)

ISBN: 978-1-911273-13-4 (hardcover)
ISBN: 978-1-911273-13-4 (softcover)
ISBN: 978-1-911273-14-1 (ebook)

Published by Mango Books
www.mangobooks.co.uk
18 Soho Square
London W1D 3QL

CONTENTS

ACKNOWLEDGEMENTS

Nicholas Connell is responsible for the inception of this book, because it was at his suggestion that I attempted it. I am very grateful for the heavy bundle of material with which he provided me forthwith, and for other many kindnesses. He is not, of course, responsible for my conclusions. Stephanie Bilton's inspirational genealogical and further suggestions speak for themselves. My late husband, Richard Whittington-Egan, was, as ever my special adviser and confidant. Dr Jan Bondeson was a most helpful colleague. I should also like my work to stand as a memorial to the Ansell family of Tankerton Street, who suffered exceptional dark tragedies, far beyond the general hardship of the London poor in 1899.

CHAPTER ONE

A HOVEL IN BLOOMSBURY

It was the midnight hour, and the tall old house in Bloomsbury was slumbering. Upstairs, the lodgers, packed into every room, were dreaming of happier places. Down in the front basement, the range was glowing – it should not have been – and it lit up the barred windows, past which, behind the area railings, dark figures were still loping and shuffling as if it were daytime. Ruffians, roisterers, gangs of youths, prostitutes, other night workers, homeless drifters and burglars were using the thoroughfare to cut across from St Pancras to Tottenham Court Road and the West End.

Inside, in the hot, stuffy kitchen, a dark-haired girl, dishevelled, was making a cake and filling it with a paste that was unnaturally yellow. It was rather late for baking, and she was far from proficient, but it would do – a smallish, flattish sponge, not well risen. She was trying to be quiet, so that she did not wake her married employers in their own room nearby. They were unlikely to come in, since the kitchen also served as her bedroom. There were advantages – privacy, which she had not been used to, access to food, and warmth, too much of it in the summer.

She packed the cake in brown paper, and addressed it laboriously in a crude, sloping hand that was purposely not quite her own. After she had washed and put away the utensils, she doused the fire, hid the cooling parcel, and clambered into the bed in which, on the Scottish principle of the servant's recessed 'jaw-box', she was expected to sleep. Now she had accomplished the preliminary stages of something that she had been planning for some months,

1

and it still seemed like a good idea. She felt no qualms.

In the morning, she would get up as usual at six o'clock and relight the range. As soon as she could slip out, she would post the parcel at the nearest post-office. There was no need to go further afield. Why should she? Everything was going to work out this time. Why not? She deserved it. A loathsome crime, against nature, *à rebours*, not unknown – it has a name – was being enacted, but Mary Ann slept soundly, oblivious of the terrible fate that was waiting for her at the end of the tunnel.

⚜

The house where Mary Ann Ansell slaved from dawn to dusk was at number 42 Great Coram Street (later plain Coram Street)[1] which linked Woburn Place to Brunswick Square. Set out in 1800 to 1804 on virgin fields belonging to the Foundling Estate, by 1899 it was lined with ranks of houses of multiple occupation, past their former glory, filled with lodgers to the attics, but performing a useful function before the bed-sitters of the twentieth century. The whole of Bloomsbury at the turn of the century was in a transitional stage. Thomas Burke, writing in 1939, saw it as 'a notable example of the whirligig of favour. From the twenties to the sixties of last century it was the home of the comfortable middle-class – the professions, banking, and commerce, with a few titles. Then, in the eighties and nineties, it began to wilt, and the comfortable deserted it for fairer quarters. The streets whose houses had been homes became nests of lodging-houses for hard-up clerks, or nests of the sorrier sort of bordello.'[2] When the young Bloomsbury Group began to colonise the better squares, their elders disapproved, warning that the district was unsafe, not properly policed.

In 1871, Great Coram Street had already gained notoriety, when, at number 12, there was a cruel and unsolved murder. Harriet Buswell, who was twenty-seven, lodged there in the second-floor back room.

---

1 Original building no longer present.
2 Thomas Burke, *Living in Bloomsbury* (London: Allen & Unwin, 1939), p. 12.

Her understanding landlady turned a blind eye when from time to time she took a man upstairs. It was all a matter of her rent. When she could find work as a dancer, she was a member of the corps-de-ballet, but there were no benefits to help her when she was 'resting'. Her one love-child had been farmed out. Thousands of women – servants on low wages, girls in seasonal jobs – were virtually part-time prostitutes, keeping afloat and assessing the risks as they came to them. That Christmas, Harriet's stranger for the night, a dark foreigner, bought her trust with half a sovereign and a net of apples and oranges and then cut her throat in the lonely, locked room. He left behind a clue – one of the apples with a bite mark – his – but was never brought to justice.

Mary Ann was not in that beleaguered category. She was well established in a permanent place and had the backing of a large family situated less than half a mile away. Her name itself was often bestowed upon maids in fiction and fact and was a foretoken of her station in life. Her technical job-description was 'general domestic servant', *vulgatim* skivvy, slavey, general, or maid of all work, and the rank was very low indeed. Her lot was to be the sole servant, as was widespread where there was not enough income to employ more help even though the work load was punishing. General domestic servant in a lodging or boarding house (not to be confused with a common lodging house, a rough expedient for the homeless, most famously in Whitechapel a shelter for the lowest prostitutes) was notoriously the hardest position of all and the least desirable. Being at the beck and call of perhaps fifteen lodgers[3] and carrying trays up and down stairs for boarders who paid for meals, keeping all the rooms clean and decent, was a task without end, lasting at least twelve hours a day. Sometimes cooking was included. Even if they began with reasonable health, especially if, much prized, they

---

3   'One of the most trying situations for a maid of all work is in a house where there are lodgers. She will, very likely, have to take everything at once to every body at once. She will be having the first and the two-pair back clamouring at the same time for the only tea-pot in the house, while the parlour will be calling angrily for his boots, which have been taken by mistake to the garret... ' Punch's *Guide to Servants*, July to December, 1845.

came from the country, the girls' health tended to deteriorate, with ailments such as anaemia and tuberculosis.

Mary Ann in Great Coram Street, looking after seventeen rooms, including her bedroom/kitchen, but spared the cooking, was not unusually martyred. Nearby establishments in the same street and of similar size employed only one struggling girl. There was no legal provision to protect servants' rights. As a matter of fact, Mary Ann's wage was exactly the same as a maid would earn in a grand, ducal house - £13 per year, 'all found', a sum which she had probably reached by annual increments. Unlike her better placed co-workers, she had not been unfairly forced to save up to buy her own uniform. A drab apron was good enough for her lowly duties.

Domestic servants, beset with chronic dissatisfaction, kept moving on to 'better' themselves, using agencies or word-of-mouth introductions, but there must have been some symbiotic connection between Mary Ann and her employers, Mr and Mrs Molony, because she had stayed with them for about five years. Nor had there been any question of her dismissal. By the end of the century, the supply of those fresh, rosy-cheeked girls from the country had begun to dry up, and, anyway, it was not easy to attract maids to the lodging houses. Mary Ann must have been doing something right, because if she had proved to be grossly unsuitable she would have jeopardised the Molonys' livelihood. There might have been an element of the devil you know. There is evidence that they were not unkind to her and allowed her considerable latitude.

From Mary Ann's point of view, there was a major compensation for the life of drudgery which was all that she knew: the proximity of her family. On her half-days off, she could walk over to see them, and her brothers and sisters were allowed to visit her in the kitchen. She was not homesick. Moreover, the West End was dangerously, temptingly close. She liked clothes and could look in the shop windows. Girls of her class dressed in hand-me-downs. She had enough time-off, in snatches, to read penny-novelettes. And there was food. There had never been enough food at home. She was obviously trusted in the kitchen, but some employers were horribly parsimonious. In the Croydon poisoning case of 1928, Mrs Noakes, the sole servant, was not permitted to take soup, and the Symington soup powders which were added to thin stock or water were doled out one by one to her, like gold.

The Ansell family, a large tribe, intermarrying with Rowleys and Randalls, similarly wide-spreading, inhabited a part of Bloomsbury which was like another country, with low crime and drunkenness. A notorious slum, little remembered today, its noxious dwellings were being swept away around the centennial transition. Lying in the north-east corner of Bloomsbury proper, bounded at the top by the Euston Road, and to the east by Gray's Inn Road, at its core was Cromer Street, infamous with its grimy courts – little sprouting by-ways. The cramped hovels had no damp-course and sewage ran underneath the floor-boards. Contagious diseases were rife, and the Irish navvies who were constructing King's Cross Station in the 1850s were said to be bringing in smallpox as they lodged in the neighbourhood. Landlords exacting rent for sub-standard dwellings were seen as rapacious. Demolition late in the nineteenth century brought further hardship, with homelessness. St Pancras Workhouse, not far away, to the north of Euston Road, was in walking distance or could be reached by a cart to take the infirm. The Metropolitan Asylums took thousands of others who could not survive on the streets.

The Ansells lived in extreme poverty, just keeping a primitive roof over their heads, finding menial and casual work when it was available, with the women and children supplementing the meagre income by street hawking. It was impossible for them to thrive and advance before welfare measures began to help them in the twentieth century. Philanthropic endeavours operated meanwhile in districts of this type.

Mrs Humphry Ward, the novelist, made provision for physically handicapped children neglected in the Bloomsbury slums, her 'cripples' on crutches, and, in 1897 opened up her Passmore Edwards Settlement in Tavistock Place to the hundreds of local children who were locked out of their homes until their parents returned home late from work.

Mary Ann's family, who were in conspicuous need, were well known to their local church and to the new school in Manchester Street, which was north of, and roughly parallel with Cromer Street, both running across to Gray's Inn Road. The Board School was the only beacon to promise any kind of escape. The schools taught the Three Rs admirably and they also improved the girls' domestic skills, not, sadly already in place from such poor homes, in order to make them employable. The children usually left school between the ages of twelve to fourteen, and sometimes the girls stayed at home for a year or so, helping their mothers, before going into their first job.

Mary Ann's family moved from one street to another when they had no option. In the 1890s, Housing Associations transformed abject lives with newly built flats for the poor, all over London, but the Ansells obviously never qualified, even supposing that they bothered to apply. They were probably too poor to keep up the rent. Her parents, James and Sarah, began their married life at number 4 Catel Place, a short *cul-de-sac* of several 'cottages' – not of the quaint rustic kind. There was only one water-closet with a water cistern above, and in 1866 the *Medical Times and Gazette* (February 3rd) reported that 'the traps were broken and the complaints of the smell from the drains were numerous.' In 1884, numbers 1 to 8 Catel Place were condemned by the St Pancras Sanitary Committee, together with other similar dwellings in Cromer Street, Gray's Inn Road and Brunswick Square. The areas complained of were described as 'fever dens', 'plague spots', and 'a vile, filthy colony.'[4]

James Ansell, Mary Ann's father, born in 1853 in Marylebone, was of Hereford stock.[5] He married Sarah Rowley, of about the same

4   A caretaker's house was 'the most disgraceful of the lot. The staircases were dark and the stairs so ricketty that it was surprising they had not fallen long ago.' Mr Nathan Robinson (Chairman of the Sanitary Committee) 'had entered the caretaker's room and when he did he found the stench so abominable that he rushed out again.'
5   Mary Ann's paternal grandmother, Caroline, born in Marylebone in 1826, married George Ansell, born in Hereford in 1824. Although a severe epileptic, Caroline managed to deliver six live children: Elizabeth, Mary Ann ('our' Mary Ann's aunt), James ('our' Mary Ann's father), George, Martha and an infant. Aunt Mary Ann brought up her family in close proximity to number 4 Catel Place, at number 1. Her husband was John Rowley, a hawker of baskets and mats, whom she married in October 1873, the same year as the

age, in 1873 (October Quarter). Both parties gave their address as 4 Catel Place, which was also the home of Sarah's parents, William and Margaret Rowley (née Randall). William was a general hawker and later a costermonger. By the time that Mary Ann was born, that is, on November 18th, 1877, James, at that stage a gas labourer, had moved his family to 75 Cromer Street itself, the hub of the deprived area. She was not the first-born. Margaret Caroline, always called Caroline, came first, on December 20th, 1873 and however normal she may have seemed as an infant – if that were so – she was eventually classified as an 'imbecile', with epilepsy. Babies continued to be born until 1898 and they were all loved and reared without childhood death from disease, a real achievement considering their living conditions. The point has been well made that in very squalid housing with minimal privacy, such as in the case of parents and six

union of James and Sarah Ansell, 'our' Mary Ann's parents. Four out of ten of their children, 'our' Mary Ann's cousins, appear to have lived: Mary Ann, William, Harriett (Parish) and Elizabeth.

On the maternal side, 'our' Mary Ann's great-grandparents were John Rowley, born in 1795 and Sarah Phillips, born in 1801. They married in St Pancras in 1822. In 1851 they were living at 14 Pancras Place; John was a hawker, and Sarah was a washerwoman. The eldest of their twelve children was William Rowley who married Margaret Randall. These were Mary Ann's grandparents. William was a railway labourer in 1851, living at 6 Clarence Court, then in 1861, a street hawker, at 5 Clarence Court, a general hawker in 1871, at 4 Catel Place, and, in 1881, at the same address, a costermonger. William and Margaret Rowley had six children before they married in 1858 and had two more children, daughters. These final girls, Margaret Harriett (born 1860) and Harriett Caroline (born 1863) were both 'insane'. They lived at home with their parents, shown at 4 Catel Place in 1871, and Harriett alone was still there in 1881. Margaret seems to have met with a catastrophe when she was 19: St Pancras workhouse records show that an illegitimate child was born there on January 8th, 1879 to a Margaret Rowley, and she was named Harriett Caroline Rowley. Sarah Rowley, Mary Ann's mother, born c. 1854, was the fourth child of the eight born to William and Margaret Rowley. Therefore, the two insane younger girls were Sarah's sisters, and Mary Ann's aunts. By a curious interconnection, John Rowley (1838-1905) a 'horse-keeper', who was one of William Rowley's younger brothers, married, in 1879, James Ansell's younger sister, Martha Ansell (born 1859). That means that Martha Ansell married her brother's wife's uncle. They produced more cousins for 'our' Mary Ann: Frederick, George, Ellen, Martha, Rosina, Albert, Ernest and Arthur. Family addresses were 7 Cantlowes Road, Camden Town in 1911, and ten years previously, 6 Union Terrace, St Pancras. Another line of cousins came from the union of Elizabeth Ansell, (born c.1846) the eldest of James Ansell's siblings, with George Miland (born 1843), a hawker, and in 1871 they were living in Suffolk Street, St Pancras. Two children were traced: William (born 1869) and Elizabeth (born 1870).

children found existing in a kitchen, all ravaged by smallpox, there was little opportunity for a woman to use fancy methods of birth control.[6] Coitus interruptus, which was free, and could be practised surreptitiously, was popular, depending on the relationship between the parties.

After Mary Ann came James (1880), Martha (1882), Emma (1884), Louisa (1887), and Florence (1889). Finally, by some device of Nature, there was a provision of boys – John (1892), William (1895), and Frederick (1898). All the children were christened at the Church of the Holy Cross in the parish of St Pancras, actually located in Cromer Street, and they had a Christian upbringing. By 1881, James had transferred his small but growing family to 21 Wood Street, also known as Midhope Street, a tributary running from Cromer Street to North Place, now Argyle Walk. He was still a labourer at the gas works: Caroline, aged seven, was at school, Mary Ann was three and James was a one-year-old. Then, number 91 Cromer Street was home at least from 1887 to 1889. James had changed drastically to working as a 'carman', driving vehicles moving goods around – less strenuous than labouring all day long, but still hard, with very long hours and exposure to all weathers. Chest complaints and rheumatism were common. There was too much waiting about and the job was not even well paid.

In 1891, in yet another change, the Ansells with seven children had three rooms at number 1, Dutton Street, which similarly went from Cromer Street to North Place. Caroline, at seventeen, had no occupation, while Mary Ann, thirteen, was already a domestic servant, probably employed locally, but still living at home. Dutton Street had for years had a bad reputation and the slums there were being cleared. In 1892, the East End Dwelling Company, founded in Whitechapel in 1882 to provide decent, affordable housing for the working poor, having demolished most of Dutton Street, put up flats which can still be seen, and the street was renamed Tankerton Street, a reference to Tankerton, in Kent, where the Company held

6   The point has been well made by Joan Perkin in *Victorian Women* (London: John Murray, 1993), p. 69.

property. For some reason, numbers 1 and 2 Dutton Street were not consumed into the spanking new flats, and, after suffering from the building works, the Ansells found themselves marooned on the edge of a new landscape, with a confusing new address of number 1 Tankerton Street. That was the last family home that Mary Ann ever knew.

Education was already over for the two eldest girls, but they had undoubtedly benefited. Even Caroline had been taught to read and write. Classes were large at the new Board Schools[7] and discipline was strict. Canings persisted in the primary schools deep into the twentieth century. The Manchester Street School, a substantial, grim building, set on a large plot of land, had been opened in 1879 to 1880, (records vary) three years after Mary Ann's birth. All of James Ansell's children are recorded as pupils at Manchester Street, except Caroline who was the eldest, and ready for school before 1880. It has not been possible to trace the school which she did attend, but she was definitely listed as a scholar on the census, which is an indication for our purposes, and the letters which she wrote were in the same style as Mary Ann's.

This was before the setting up of Special Schools at the turn of the century.[8] The acceptance of 'imbecile' children into mainstream schools was the norm, although as these children flocked into the classrooms around 1880, their special needs were certainly noticed by those in authority. By 1898, there were already classes for 'mentally deficient' pupils under the London School Board, which, in 1900, decreed that children of normal intelligence were not to be

---

7   Although we might suppose, nostalgically, that the Board School teachers, duly 'certificated' were treated with grateful respect by parents, themselves of little education, this was by no means always the case. For example, an 'irate mother', Mrs Harrington, of number 6 Loxham Houses, Loxham Street, Gray's Inn Road, was summoned in May, 1899, for assaulting Thomas Elgie, an assistant master at Manchester Street School. She drew a cane concealed in her cloak and struck him two blows, in retaliation for a caning which he had administered to one of her sons. She was bound over to be of good behaviour and reminded that a teacher's work was very hard.

8   The Elementary Education (Defective and Epileptic Children) Act of 1899 empowered local authorities to set up special schools and classes, and to force parents of children diagnosed as needing special education on account of mental handicap to send them to appropriate schools. Non-compliance could incur the large fine of £5.

taught with such children. The wheel turned in the later twentieth century, with an ideal of 'inclusion' of mentally handicapped children, and the Special Schools, which had once been considered a model of enlightenment, were run down and reduced in number. Caroline will not have been the only pupil in her class who was slow to learn.

Elementary education for all children became compulsory and compellable by the hated attendance officers in 1880. Shameful decades of strife and resistance from some sections of the ruling classes, as well as the Church, had passed before the plight of pauper children was addressed for all time. Pure philanthropy had fought for many years against vested interests. Only the material realisation that the work force was handicapped in its productivity by its illiteracy, where other countries had made better provision of education in the new industrial climate and reaped the benefits, seems to have prevailed. Many poor parents resented the great change, especially when there was a charge of a penny or so per child, but that was abolished in 1891. There is every indication that James and Sarah appreciated the great benefit: they themselves were illiterate, having missed out.

The lodging house in Great Coram Street where Mary Ann settled down, followed at least one other residential job. Before that period, when she was about fourteen years old, she was sent up north to Yorkshire, probably by some arrangement stemming from her school. Far from home, in a rural environment, she seemed to have done all right as a maid at Crow Nest, Dewsbury. This was a large mansion of sixteenth to seventeenth century origins, owned in Victorian times by the Haque family. In 1893, the house and estate were sold to Dewsbury Corporation and possibly that was the reason for Mary Ann's return to her roots in Bloomsbury, which was a pity, because she was said to have been well thought of there. At Great Coram Street, she acquired a certain pertness and urban confidence, but ultimately it did her no favours. No doubt there was badinage with the clerks, telegraphists and shop assistants whom she served, all young men, whose wages were not that much better than hers.

The Molonys, her Bloomsbury employers, were both of Irish origin, coming from Clare, County Clare. At first, Margaret Stritch, as she then was, ran the house on her own account, taking only gentleman lodgers. Once she had a superior boarder, Arthur Wood, a classics teacher. Patrick John Molony was one of the eight lodgers in 1891, a tailor, aged twenty-five, working all hours like everyone else around him in the fight to stay solvent and in good health. Margaret Stritch's age tended to vary over the years: she was in fact some five years older than Patrick. Anyway, Patrick and Margaret married in 1893, and two children, William and Kathleen were born in 1895/6. This means that Mary Ann was trusted to be in daily contact with two young children.

In 1892, when Mary Ann was fifteen, a great sadness visited the Ansell household. James was the first son born to James and Sarah and loved as they all were in their turn. He had his time at Manchester Street School, but his short life ended suddenly when he was twelve, as the result of an horrific railway accident. His mother said later that Caroline was perfectly normal before the shock of losing her brother. That was palpably not the case, but people have always seized upon false reasons for mental illness.

The Victorians were entranced by their powerful steam-trains, but were also scared of them. Railway disasters received extensive press coverage with all gory detail minutely described. This particular event came cruelly on Easter Monday, when the town workers and their children were transported by the London and North Western Line to the famous Bank Holiday Fair on Hampstead Heath. There was green countryside, and there were music pavilions and it was springtime. At 6 o'clock in the evening, when the stalls were closing, James Ansell made for home, via the Hampstead Heath Railway Station. He had three friends with him: James Gorrie (12) of 67 Cromer Street, Alfred Charles Lathey (13) of 87 Cromer Street, and Charles Holloway (12) of 90 Cromer Street. None of the four schoolboys would have had much money, if any at all, to spend, but it had been a great adventure, and their last one. None of them reached home.

Hundreds of people were descending on the small station, as they always did at Easter time, but suddenly there were black clouds and a downpour coming, and the crowds rushed in for shelter under the station roof. The staircase to the up-platform was rather narrow and obstructed by the ticket-office and something went wrong. Perhaps someone tripped, and the gate at the bottom might have been wrongly closed. Many theories were advanced, but the fact was that hundreds poured down into a bottle-neck and adults and children were crushed to death. Some people managed to cross the line and infants were tossed to safety. Eight died on the spot – two women and six boys. *The Times* (April 26th) reported that the funerals of James Ansell and Alfred Charles Lathey would take place on that day:

> The street in which these poor lads lived runs from Gray's Inn Road into Judd Street, Euston Road, and is very thickly populated by people belonging to the working class. At nearly every house the blinds were drawn yesterday during the time of the funerals, and a very large number of spectators assembled to see the start made for the cemetery. The shops in the neighbourhood had shutters up, and at a public house at the corner a flag floated at half-mast. The traffic was regulated by police under the direction of Divisional-Inspector Everett, of the E Division. The procession from the house in which the parents of Gorrie lived was the first to start. It was headed by police until it had passed into the Gray's Inn Road, whence it proceeded quietly on its way to Finchley Cemetery.

Young James was the first of Sarah's brood to leave just a memory in the cramped, dark rooms in Tankerton Street, and she mourned him for the rest of her life.

Worse was to come: an accident, like flood and tempest, was natural, an act of God, but her family were supposed to stick together, not throw the weakest one out of the nest.

CHAPTER TWO

A PLACE OF SAFETY

Poor Caroline's last sight of home was in October, 1894, when she was torn from her family in Tankerton Street and removed by the Relieving Officer to the Leavesden Metropolitan Asylum for Pauper Idiots and Imbeciles, near Watford, in Hertfordshire.[9]

In spite of her elementary education, she had turned out to be unemployable, and was a burden to her parents, with worsening behaviour. Her epileptic fits, uncontrolled, must have become intolerable in the cramped household with young children. Best practice, now regarded as downright cruel, was to displace both 'lunatics' and 'imbeciles' from their urban roots to the care of the large asylum which served their particular catchment area, on the opposite side of their patch. It was more difficult for them to try to get home; they did not know where they were; the travel provisions were mysterious; and home was pathogenic, anyway. These arrangements caused hardship for many years. If the asylum could be placed in a pastoral setting, that was even more therapeutic. Romantic eighteenth and nineteenth century notions

---

9   There are a considerable number of full volumes on individual asylums, often written by previous staff and informed by a touching nostalgia, but none on Leavesden. However, several interesting pamphlets are held at Hertfordshire Archives, and have been drawn upon for matters of fact for this present study (see Select Bibliography). Monica Diplock, in her excellent short *The History of Leavesden Hospital* (one of the pamphlets) had access to some archives but, unfortunately, there was a severe flood in the 1970s which entered the basement store where many case notes, grave records and other material were kept, and destroyed them. Former patients' memories of asylums in general tend to be critical and unforgiving. Was Leavesden one of the 'whited sepulchres full of dry bones', or was it a palace of enlightenment?

about the healing power of Nature lay queasily under the medical and logistical necessities. The dark city, a den of iniquity, riddled with vice, a carbuncle, its gutters running with filth, was thought of as a cause of madness in itself. Small, private 'retreats', such as Ticehurst, in Sussex, with its gardens and aviary of gold and silver pheasants, established the model. 'Out of sight. Out of mind' was undoubtedly a covert factor, especially when handicap was severe.

The culture shock for the transported was disregarded, the vast wards and day-rooms, the moving mass of disordered strangers, causing the feeling later identified as *anomie*, of being lost and unattached, as if your own symptoms were not bad enough. Many poor people, like the Ansells, could only rarely, if ever, afford the expense of travelling to visit their incarcerated relatives. If the asylum were St Lawrence's, the South Eastern Railway Company allowed a forty per cent reduction in third class tickets for people visiting the inmates. The inclination to make the journey tended to fade over the years, so that the rescued one was trapped in isolation, although paradoxically and claustrophobically never alone.

Caroline was able, on occasion, to contact her family by writing to them – a new accomplishment for the younger asylum dweller – but, it was noted, rarely spoke of home. After five years she had drifted away from them, a familiar story. The shame of having a family member confined was often a discouragement. James and Sarah were not bad parents: they loved all their children without exception, but circumstances were against them. Although she did show some improvement, Caroline had little hope of discharge. Some people did get out. Her basic mental disability was permanent, and she could not realistically be returned to her former environment. Nor could she walk out, because at that time all the inmates of the 'Idiot and Imbecile' Asylums were held under certificate, by virtue of the Lunacy Acts. An escapee would be returned in disgrace.

Leavesden took from London north of the Thames, while, neatly, south of the Thames was served by St Lawrence's, at Caterham, Surrey. The idea that subnormality required separate institutions came in a laggardly way after the great County Lunatic Asylums were set up by the Lunacy Act of 1845. These sister Metropolitan Asylums, both opened in 1870, were designed by the same architect, and of the same large size. The Victorians liked their significant buildings and assets to be big, and did not perceive that their plan of collecting 1500 inmates in one enormous macrocosm, with everyone tamed and functioning like automata for the common good, was imperfect.

By contrast, in the 'lunatic asylums', there was an assumption that effective medical treatment was appropriate, expected, and offered, which in some wards created a different, less hopeless and mechanical ambiance, however dubious the therapies that were administered. At least the unfortunates – the 'imbeciles' – were not messed about with, not half-drowned, electrocuted, bled, infected with malaria, or leucotomised. Not much thought or discussion was expended on the subject of mental defect although the housing of such patients was earnestly debated. Medical treatment for them was sparse, but as a matter of fact was never plentiful in the large lunatic asylums. Non paupers were seen more often by a doctor in the private asylums to which they were supposed to be sent, unless the place turned out to be an abusive one. That was where the Commissioners in Lunacy came in. The dosing of epileptics with bromides was one specific proven measure at institutions.

The newly-formed Metropolitan Asylums Board calculated that three-thousand 'imbecile' beds were sufficient for the whole of London, but, as happened with the 'lunatic' asylums, the estimate was too low. The inmates of both types of asylums poured in when the relief was offered, traditionally, especially in rural areas, from shuttered attics, but actually mostly from the workhouses, themselves large collectives in their lunatic wards. Chronicity began to clog up the beds. That is well-known, but hindsight is glib. The highest philanthropic ideals informed the desire to improve the lot of the mentally ill and handicapped. Reformers did not like to see them miserable and vulnerable in the workhouses, where special consideration varied according to the management, nor to see them wandering the streets in rags and hungry. Unlike the workhouses, the costs of Leavesden and St Lawrence's came out of the rates, not central government, and there was a pressure to justify the drain on the common pocket. Cost-factoring sat uneasily with spiritual views of the improvement of the mental health of the paupers who did not fit into society.

So it was, on Saturday, October 31st, 1868, that, in an effusion of benevolence, a gaggle of very important persons assembled on the platform at Euston to board their special train to Watford, where omnibuses were waiting. The occasion was described in lyrical terms: a pleasant drive through winding by-ways fringed with yellow frondage of beech-trees and darker leaves of oak. Sycamores rustled their branches or fell like 'Imperial Jove' in a golden shower to the earth. Past Lord Essex' Tudor gate lodge, past the lately-restored Early-English church at Leavesden village, with crosses dotting the green sward of God's acre, the horses pulled into their collars up a steep, narrow lane to the site of the new asylum. The ground sloped upward behind the proposed building, and in front there was an extensive view as far as Harrow.

The visitors alighted and formed themselves into a procession which solemnly perambulated the exposed foundations, and then encircled the foundation stone – a fine block of Portland, with an inlaid tablet of Sicilian marble, bearing the names of the committee of the Metropolitan Asylums Board. An awning had been erected over a platform, which accommodated the visiting dignitaries, the choir of Abbots Langley church, and the band of the Coldstream Guards. There were prayers, and psalms.

Dr Brewer, Chairman of the Board, addressed the company in reassuring terms: they had all met there that day to mark the formation of an asylum for those poor people whom mental affliction had incapacitated for the duties of life – those who had cause to be regarded with one feeling, that of hearty commiseration. The stone was lowered to rest over a sealed bottle, which contained coins of the reigning Queen, a list of the managers of the Board, a copy of the relevant Act of Parliament, and *The Times* newspaper. The military band played, from Elijah, 'O rest in the Lord'. There were more prayers, and hymns, and, at last, an elegant *déjeuner*, served by

Messrs Staples, of the Albion. There were toasts, in a more relaxed atmosphere, with speeches which contained thoughts which would have offended later audiences. The Bishop of Rochester remarked that he could bear witness from his experience as chaplain to the Kidderminster workhouse that this was the very charity most wanted in the country, because it would relieve the infirm from the infliction of the presence of the imbecile. The Earl of Verulam thanked God that they were about to make provision for their humbler fellow-subjects, who, as they were now placed, added to the misery of others. They could not prevent the affliction, but they might relieve it. He hoped for greater relief from medical advance, and also he begged for temperance, so as to dry up to a great extent the source of that evil they were trying to remedy – which unscientific assertion was received with resounding cheers. Drunkenness was widely believed and ratified by the medical profession as the cause of the birth of mentally defective children in the poor classes – a pernicious fallacy.

After a long day, the refreshed benevolent party departed to return to London at 5.30 p.m. The field with its bare foundations fell silent until Monday, when heavy building work tore up the soil and a massive edifice began to emerge, an alien, mushrooming structure in the virgin countryside. The blocks of Nottingham and Leicester red and yellow bricks,[10] quite decorative, and paler in effect than many of the red, castellated Tudor style county asylums, spread incongruously over the fields. The whole was designed on the 'Pavilion System',[11] to be seen also in St Thomas's Hospital in London, which was all about ventilation and separation of units so that fresh air could circulate unimpeded. More women than men were expected, with six female blocks and five male. Each held

10 Constructed of new bricks, coloured cream to sandy, or near white as they mellowed, ornamented with linear red bricks or denser red patterning, not designed to be towering or overpowering, the architecture was almost playful and meant to please, to make light of a necessity, a more benevolent and spiritual refuge than a workhouse. The sheer, repetitive number of the identical blocks in this fanciful style was perhaps quite bizarre.
11 *The Builder*, July 25th, 1868, carried detailed plans of Leavesden and continued its coverage until the building was established.

eighty residents, with the ground floor intended as a day-room and the upper two stories as dormitories.

The 'lunatic' and the 'imbecile' asylums shared the same absolutely recognisable architecture, with their own particular stylistic idiosyncrasies, and were indistinguishable from the exterior. On the whole, the general public understood the difference of the two functions, although, confusingly, the term 'lunatic' was often used indiscriminately, even by people with special knowledge. Once inside Leavesden, the lesser reliance on security became apparent. Only four special rooms per ward were set aside for disturbed inmates, whereas whole refractory wards were designated at the lunatic asylums, where violence was expected.

The plan was that if a harmless 'imbecile' became too difficult to manage in the lenient Leavesden environment, as certainly could happen, or was revealed after admission to be less controllable than described, then he would be transferred to a county asylum, where cases of that type were already, undoubtedly, housed. There was bound to be an interfusion, and, as time passed, the county asylums transferred harmless 'burnt-out' psychotics no longer in need of strict confinement to places like Leavesden. Aaron Kosminski, the Ripper suspect was moved there from Colney Hatch in 1894 when his 'mania' had subsided. Attendants at the asylums where aggression to them was an everyday occurrence were better paid and some brave souls would change their job for that reason. At first, there were no iron bars on the windows at Leavesden, until someone escaped by that route in about 1881.

Leavesden in 1870 was new and shining, a modern marvel, designed and equipped to the hilt with the latest models of heating, ventilation, workshops and kitchenalia, everything jumbo-size. The wards filled up quickly, the bewildered new inmates arriving in batches from the railway station by horse-drawn vans, rather as the 'lunatics' from Bedlam were transferred to the newly erected Broadmoor in its own green seclusion. Work, holy work, was the mainspring of the regime, a clockwork routine to even out disordered minds. It was not so much an early 'therapeutic community' as a cooperative, all working for the common good in a self-sufficient stockade. There was no opportunity for formal occupational therapy; that would be important later on. In the workhouses, notoriously, labour was forced, to encourage the others and deter reliance on the state, but the daily grind in the asylums to which those fit to work were directed, as if there were no alternative, must have been ruefully contemplated by those capable of making comparisons. For the women, slaving without payment in the laundries and kitchens, scrubbing the ward floors and staircases with raw, red hands was not really humane and indeed later proscribed. There were some refuseniks who petitioned for return to the workhouse, where, they said, they were not entirely surrounded by lunatics, and where they were near their families and friends. The asylum was a Christian machine, with its chapel built in a central position, the polished pews seating six hundred as the chaplain preached on duty, charity and forgiveness.

The men fared better, on the whole, working on the model farm or in the workshops, with all products for the benefit of the community. There was an asylum bull – a speckled Ayrshire – and he had a job to do to keep his place. The staff worked twelve-hour shifts. At the apex of the whirring turbine, the medical superintendents of the public asylums, oppressed by administration and the demand for economy, were prone to suffer their own brand of burn-out. How sad the gulf between the early days of exaltation as the first footings were laid, and the final demolition of the bricks in the second half of the next century.

When Caroline Ansell was admitted in 1894, she was from then on a figure of no significance whatsoever, deposited in a long day-room, lofty with iron pillars holding up the two dormitory floors above. There was no privacy, but she was used to that at home, required to sleep beside thirty other restless souls, the narrow beds set out in two rows, close together. A bed of her own was a luxury, everything clean and neat, not damp and cold, with four fireplaces to each dormitory. They bathed her and whisked away her own thin clothes before the anonymous costume of cap, shawl and dress was allotted to her. The female attendants were strict, and wore prison-like uniforms with their name and number. Thirty per cent of the inmates suffered from epilepsy as a feature of their mental defect, and their fits added fevered, sudden movement to the subdued conformity. There was an effort to concentrate those with epilepsy in one ward with extra staffing, and certainly Caroline was in Ward 7, the female ward for epileptics, although she might have been placed randomly at first, wherever a bed had become vacant.

She had never known such luxury, kept clean with a weekly bath, her clothing and bedding regularly washed, and nourishing food, lots of it, regularly appearing, set before her at one of the four tables in the ward, each seating twenty. Before, she had always been hungry, fed with watered milk, poor, adulterated bread, perhaps a bit of bacon sometimes, but now she could feast on her share of 7lb loaves of fresh bread, and butter, meat, vegetable, pies, soup, beer and tea. This Herculean fare was always home-produced, sincerely offered, and magnificently organic. It was in a different league from workhouse food, and a credit to the rate-payers. The half-starved put on weight and thrived, although infectious diseases, especially typhoid and tuberculosis could take hold.

For the first time in her life, Caroline had access to indoor lavatories off the day-room, and off the dormitory. There was a decent infirmary, but she remained physically well. The way to survive mentally, unless you were too handicapped to interact, was to form a small group of friends on your ward, to build up relationships, even at a simple level, to live with familiar faces and voices, sit with them at meal-times, talk about where you came from in London, and perhaps, not necessarily, mention your family. Caroline was well enough, and spirited enough, to do all this. The sexes were firmly segregated, of course, and the very idea of coupling was beyond the pale. Any ward is only as good as its staff, whatever the standard of the plumbing and heating, but there is surviving evidence that Caroline was treated with respect and kindness. How eagerly we scan the old group photographs of the hard-pressed staff in about 1900 for signs of proud professionalism and compassion, and seem to see them there. By 1899, the old-style attendants were ceding to a more sympathetic atmosphere, with full nursing uniform and Florence Nightingale caps: some began to take formal examinations.

The titular head of both types of asylum held a god-like status in the hierarchy and was a prominent authority figure in the delusions of the paranoid insane, and therefore a magnet for attack. Nevertheless, Medical or Physician Superintendent of a large asylum was a sought-after salaried post, a clever career choice, a worthwhile and interesting job for life, as long as you and your family were comfortable living on the premises in designated quarters, sometimes a good, solid house. The deference accorded to you in your immediate orbit might be gratifying, but some others in the medical profession scoffed at 'alienists' and 'mad doctors'. Then, as later, there were only a limited number of top jobs in the asylums, and there was a considerable turn-over of lower medical officers who might abandon psychiatric work for alternative areas. It was later that consultants with their own teams diversified the asylum culture and brought in more discussion.

In 1898, at Leavesden, the medical superintendent was still absolute king of the castle, subject to the Board. In that year, a new broom was appointed. Dr Frank Ashby Elkins (1862–1941) MB, CM, BSc, succeeded out of a large number of applicants. He had resigned in February from the position of Medical Superintendent of Ryhope Asylum, Sunderland, chosen in 1894 from fifty-nine applicants: his salary then was £350 per annum, with a furnished house, board, gas, firing, and two servants. Already in the asylum business by the age of twenty-nine, he was previously assistant physician at the Royal Asylum for the Insane in Edinburgh. He did not have a conventional medical background. His father, Joseph, who was not affluent, was a farmer, and then a grazier. He began his career as a chemist's apprentice, and qualified as a doctor in Edinburgh in 1888. His two sisters also thrived in the asylums: Louise was assistant Matron at the Royal, Edinburgh, in 1891, and Edith Anne was of the same grade at the same hospital in 1901. By 1911 she was Matron at the Scarborough Asylum, Yorkshire.

Although Medical Superintendents tended to eccentricities, became characters, wise and witty, no anecdotes along these lines have surfaced in regard to Dr Elkins. He introduced some ameliorations, and managed to appoint a third, much needed Assistant Medical Officer. Times were changing, and mechanical restraints were phased out; they were not of the gross type employed in the lunatic asylums, apparently, but intended to prevent self-harm and accidents, especially in the case of epileptics. The bare planks of the floors were now stained and polished and easier to clean. The wards were improved, with pictures, flowers and table-cloths and even caged birds. Recreational facilities were somewhat improved. Knitting needles were permitted. In the earlier days, it had been up to the Chaplain to provide a small library, the assumption being that 'imbeciles' would have no ability or desire to read books or newspapers, but that proved untrue when reading material became available although it was noticed at St Lawrence's Asylum that picture-books were particularly popular on the wards.

However, the improvements which were implemented *after the First World War* reveal how uncomfortable daily life had been for Caroline and her friends. Communal toothbrushes, hairbrushes, combs, nail-brushes and towels were now issued individually. Proper lavatory paper was provided. Some women were supplied with knickers instead of serge petticoats. The old Victorian bonnets were replaced by straw or felt hats for outdoor use.

The unwieldiness of the vast asylum caused compound stresses. By 1876, the original estimated number of places had already increased from 1,500 to 2,118 inmates actually held and new wards had to be built on to the old blocks. This was happening everywhere. Before Dr Elkins' term, Dr Walmsley, Acting Medical Superintendent, grumbled in a report dated December 1st, 1886, that,

> The asylum is becoming more and more an Infirmary, a place for stowing away all the wreckage of our social system – a place where is thrown together everything in human nature troublesome and unsightly, dotard old people, demented epileptics, helpless paralytics, deserted imbeciles, young and old, whose feeble mental faculties make unusual demands upon the resources of the poorhouse – all

are thrown into the District Asylums, whose function thus becomes mainly, if not entirely, custodial.

Outside, in the real world, in 1897, Queen Victoria celebrated her Diamond Jubilee, and at Leavesden, in the middle of nowhere, her majesty's loyal and grateful subjects, their hidden existence not on her wave-length, sat down to a grand feast of extra beef and mutton, jam roly-poly pudding, lemonade, tobacco and snuff. Otherwise, night followed day in that place of monotony and Caroline missed her family, more than they missed her. The visitors' rooms were thinly used. Sometimes she received a Christmas card. Her ward friends were her family. Her epilepsy was part of her life. An occasional picnic, or a dance, was a fleeting excitement. The slums of St Pancras grew misty in her simple mind. The staff looked after her, and she felt safe and secure.

CHAPTER THREE

'AS INNOCENT A GIRL AS EVER WAS BORN'

Five times the leaves had changed on the trees around the asylum and Christmas had come to the great communal home, the long rooms dressed with holly and the tables laden with traditional produce from the farm. Caroline was twenty-five-years-old, biddable and institutionalised, as we now see it, never leaving the grounds, dosed for her epilepsy, trudging around the airing-court (more a field) with her friends, knowing her boundaries. However, everything began to go wrong for her, when, on February 22nd, 1899, a devastating letter reached her by post from that outside world which she had lost.

> Dear Carrie, [it reads, in quite clear, sloping writing with plentiful loops] I now send these few lines to tell you that your father and mother is dead they [died] last week and I am sorry for you and they dear little ones that are left all the children sends their love to you and they hope you are quite well I think this is all at present.
>
> I remain
> Yours Cousin
> Harriett Parish

The letter was headed:

> 1 Tankerton Street
> Cromer Street,

that being the Ansell family home. Harriett, born in about 1875, was one of Caroline's first cousins on the paternal side. James Ansell's sister, another Mary Ann, had married John Rowley, a hawker of baskets and mats, and Harriett was one of their children. She married

24

Daniel Parish, a coal porter, and in 1899 they were at 3 Oslington Place, Somers Town. In 1901 they were living in very crowded conditions at 8 Derry Street, St Pancras with two daughters, Harriett (4) and Rose (9 months): Daniel was a rag sorter.

Caroline had no reason to disbelieve the blunt message of woe and it would have been a reasonable assumption that Harriett would have been around number 1 Tankerton Street at a time of disaster. The staff of Ward 7 saw that Caroline Ansell was crying, and Nurse Alice Felmingham, who was in charge, found out what had happened. Two days later, Caroline sat down at a table and wrote a letter to Harriett at 1 Tankerton Street, expressing her sorrow in the stereotypical Board School style which adequately covered most lifetime transactions.

> My dear Cousion Harriet I write these few lines to you hoping to find you and all your family all quite well and happy at home has it leaves me and all my dear friends at present and to tell you that we received your letter that you sent to us. My dear Cousion Harriet me and all my dear friends sends all our very best love to you and all the family and to tell you that we received that little parcel that you sent to us but the sugar tasted so bitterley in the tea. My dear Cousion Harriet me and all my dear friends was so very sorry to hear about dear loving Father and Mother being dead but would you mind sending me their funeral card and to tell me in the next letter what they both dyed with but we all hopes that all the dear little children will get on alright and would you mind giving them some kisses for me and all my dear friends. My dear Cousion Harriet would you mind trying to send me some black lace ribbons for to keep in morning for them but if you happen to see dear sister Polly [ie Mary Ann, possibly so called in the family to differentiate her from her aunt of the same name, Harriett's mother] would you mind giving all our very best love to her and the rest of all the others in all the family I think that this is all we can say at present but write has soon as you can and let us know if you received the letter I will now say good night and God Bless every one of you in all the family I remain your ever loving and affection Cousion Caroline Ansell-
>
> XXXXXXX XXXXXXX
> XXXXX XXXXX
> XXXXX XXXXX
> XXX XXXX
> XXX XXX
> XX XX
> X X

Kisses and love to all at home.

Again, it was a reasonable assumption that Harriett had been the anonymous donor of the parcel of tea and sugar mentioned in the letter. Under house rules, letters were passed intact to inmates, but parcels, for obvious reasons of security, had to be opened and inspected by staff. Nurse Felmingham had unwrapped the small parcel and decided that it was harmless before giving it to Caroline. Disappointment had followed when Caroline made tea, the following day. The brew was so bitter that it was undrinkable, and she was told to throw it down the sink. The sugar, which was moist, looked like ordinary yellow demerara.

When Caroline's letter addressed to Harriett Parrish was delivered, puzzlingly, to 1 Tankerton Street, James Ansell, who was present and very much alive, opened it. He had to get Emma, aged fourteen, to read it to him, and, as anyone would have been, was angry and troubled. He told Emma to write back to Caroline to say that the letter was a lie, and asking her to send it to him. Emma was also instructed to tell her that if he could find out who wrote the letter he would 'just tell them not to be so kind as to tell any more lies and he would have them put in a place where they could be taken care of.' James Ansell enclosed a newspaper and a religious tract. There followed a meeting of some kind with Harriett, who denied sending the letter and was always and absolutely believed by everyone concerned. As they discussed the identity of the malicious letter writer, who obviously had knowledge of the family, all the members of that family expressed themselves to be mystified, perhaps regarding the affair as a cruel hoax. James clearly suspected that the sender was not in a normal state of mind, and there the matter rested.

Caroline wrote home on February 28th, a joyous and touching letter in her usual cyclical style:

> My Dear Loving Father and Mother I write these few line to you hoping to find you and all the family all quite well and happy at home has it leaves me and all my dear friend at present and to tell you we received your kind and welcome letter and very please to hear from you my Dear Father and Mother me and all my dear friends sends all our very best love to you and all the family, My Dear loving Father I your dear loving daughter and all my dear friends hopes that you

and all the family has got plenty of work to do and I thank you so very much my most dear and loving Father and mother for sending me the newspaper and that pretty little book that you sent to us. Dear loving Father and Mother you ask me in your letter to send me that letter you ask me for that I got last week and it upset me and all my dear friend very much to hear that you was dead but it liven me and all my dear friend up to hear you are still alive and I have sent you that letter in this letter my most Dear ever loving Father and Mother I know that you and all the family will be very please to hear all that I am going to tell you that is me and all my dear friends are all quite well and happy to hear that you are still alive and I your dear loving daughter is still doing my work so very nicely and we are still behaving ourselves. My Dear loving Father and Mother would you mind doing a favour for me and all my dear friends that is to kiss all my dear sisters and all my dear Brothers and to wish my dear little Brother Billy a merry happ returns of the day for us all I think that is all we can say at present I will now say good night and God Bless every one of you all I remain your ever loving and affectionate Daughter Caroline Ansell.

There was a second wave of disturbance, when, on March 9th, a second parcel with no note of sender was delivered to Caroline's ward. One of the head attendants was always present when a parcel was received, and Mary Ann Hussey performed this duty. Nurse Felmingham unwrapped it, and inside the brown paper there was a cake, which she handed over to Caroline Ansell with no hesitation, apparently making no connection with the previous packet of tea and sugar. Inmates were quite often sent cakes, pastries and sweetmeats and she was very busy at the time, being in charge of a ward of 141 patients – an unreasonable task, one would have thought – with only the back-up of Nurse Mary Ann Hussey. People did not send cakes to Caroline: she came from the poorest of the poor, just above destitution, and there was no spare money for ingredients or postage. Big slabs of wholesome asylum cake were available but an individual, home-made cake was a great treat for Caroline and she was eager to share it with her friends. It was a sort of hybrid concoction; descriptions varied. Nurse Felmingham thought that it was a small piece of pastry, like a jam sandwich, about the size of ordinary note-paper and only half-an-inch thick. Mary Driscoll, one of the friends, said that it was like a turn-over cake, very hard, and very yellow. It does not seem to have looked very appetising. Nurse Felmingham also had a memory of it as like a cheesecake, with a middle substance more yellow than the rest.

Caroline, with great resolve, saved the cake until tea-time, 6.30 pm, the following day, Friday, March 10th. She ate half herself, and gave portions, which cannot have been large, since the cake was quite small, to Mary Driscoll, Mary Smithers, Kate Maloney, and Mary Maloney. At least two other women, Mary Gristwood and Mary Carey, tasted the cake that evening of the next day. Perhaps there was some casual nibbling of the remnants. It was not delicious, but it was an irresistible rarity. Kate Maloney had the sense to spit out her first mouthful because it was so bitter.

Next morning, Caroline woke up feeling bilious and with no appetite. The whites of her eyes were yellow, but she was allowed or encouraged to go about her domestic work as usual. Mary Driscoll had vomited all night and was 'bad' all day, with stomach ache and the bitter taste of the cake in her throat. She felt ill until the following Wednesday. Mary Maloney, too, was complaining of stomach ache. Caroline was worse by dinner-time, feeling sick; Nurse Felmingham removed her from the table and gave her a 'black draught' and a piece of toast, which made her vomit. At tea-time she took a little bread and butter and left the rest. They let her go to bed early. On Sunday morning, she said that she felt better, although she was still looking very yellow, but she went to church, as usual. At dinner afterwards, she kept down some beef. At 3 pm she took a cup of tea, but vomited immediately afterwards.

The reality was that a sizeable group who sat at table with Caroline Ansell and failed to do justice to the day's substantial menu of bread and butter and tea with milk for breakfast, bread and cheese for lunch, beef pie for dinner and tea and bread and butter for tea, shared gastric symptoms, and although ward notes may have been made, there was no overview at that time to suggest that there was anything seriously amiss.

Monday, 13th was Nurse Felmingham's day-off, and when she

arrived on the ward at 7.30 am on Tuesday, she found Caroline looking very ill. Her lips had turned black and her eyes were extremely peculiar. Medical attention should almost certainly have been sought on the Sunday, but now the head attendant was summoned, and Dr Matthew Cameron Blair, Assistant Medical Officer, was called. Young Dr Blair, a Scot, graduate of Glasgow University, born June 18th, 1867, in Paisley, was, like his senior, an excellent doctor, but of a more exotic and restless nature. 'He was a confirmed bachelor, and it was his pose, which deceived no one, to be something of a woman-hater.' *The Times.* Doctors of his calibre often walked the wards of the asylums, and were good company for their colleagues. *The Times* (again):

> In any society he would have commanded respect by reason of his high professional attainments, his ready classical scholarship, and his love of good literature. But the key to the universal affection that he inspired lay rather in his transparent singleness of heart, his disregard of worldly trappings, his gaiety, his camaraderie, and above all his genius for friendship.

This, then, was the highly qualified and characterful doctor whom they led at 8 am to the suffering figure seated, not lying, on a sofa in the long ward. He saw at once that she had what was called an 'abdominal face', drawn with anguish. She said that she had a bad pain. Her tongue was dry and furred, and she was showing signs of shock. She could scarcely speak. Recognising that she was seriously ill, he had her transferred without delay to the women's infirmary, numbered 1a. Here at last in a hospital bed with close medical supervision and infirmary staff, Caroline was at the very least more comfortable and, one would have thought, had a chance of recovery. She was young and strong, well fed and used to hard work. Emily Collyer, the nurse in charge, put her to bed when she arrived in great pain at 8.25. She had a headache and nausea. She said, and this is the first recorded evidence that what was wrong was being recognised, that she had eaten some cake on Friday, and had not been well since.

Back on ward 7, Mary Maloney's pains passed off, and Mary Driscoll improved after being sick. Mary Smithers kept on vomiting, but was not moved. Dr Blair continued to monitor his patient, Caroline Ansell, who was very ill. By noon, she was still quite conscious and appeared 'collected', but had virtually lost the power of speech. By the evening, although still conscious, she was mute, and her abdomen was grossly distended. Dr Blair did all that he could for her and last saw her at about 7.40 pm, when she was dying. Nurse Collyer was at her side when she died at 8 o'clock in the evening, after only one day in the infirmary. The date was March 14th.

At that time, Dr Blair's opinion was that peritonitis (a grave diagnosis in those days) was the cause of death. He had been told that Caroline had been eating cake, before her illness, but to that *he attached no importance because he knew that cakes were frequently sent to patients.*

As for 'the woman Smithers', *when he was first called to her on March 15th* he thought that she was suffering from a bilious attack, such as she had had before; and he prescribed for her accordingly. She did not appear to him to be ill enough for the infirmary. He had a look at her again in her dormitory that evening, and admitted her to the infirmary on the morning of the 16th, with symptoms of disordered liver and stomach. Eventually, she recovered. She told Dr Blair about the cake, and he did think that there might have been something in it that had caused illness.

Anxious, by now, and no doubt there were rumours, Dr Blair consulted Dr Elkins, Medical Superintendent, and they decided on a post-mortem. They wrote to the Ansells, to ask for their permission – a formal requirement. News of the death had been sent to them by a special notice from the asylum steward, and they had received it on the 15th. On March 16th, with help from the church poor-box or others marginally better-off than themselves, Caroline's mother, Sarah, and her sister, Mary Ann, travelled by train to see the body at the asylum. At last they came to her in death, not in life, which would have meant so much to her.

Dr Blair saw them and told Mrs Ansell that her daughter had died somewhat suddenly. It had come to his knowledge that she had eaten some cake, and another patient who had partaken of the cake was also ill. The mother denied all knowledge of any cake. She was weeping, but there was a strange anger about Mary Ann.

Dr Blair said that because of the suspicious combination of circumstances he was constrained to ask Mrs Ansell's permission for a post-mortem, but she refused outright, being without her husband's support. She promised to discuss it with James and get him to reply by the evening post.

Edward Farmer was the porter on duty as Sarah and Mary Ann were leaving by the asylum gate, and his kindness to the bereaved was quite remarkable. He saw that Mary Ann was 'broken down' and 'unhinged'. She asked him how to obtain a death certificate for her sister and he immediately offered to write a letter for her there and then to the Registrar at Rickmansworth. She signed it, and he posted it. When she asked him about an insurance policy certificate, he told her that it would cost 2s 7d, and she said that she would send the money. They went home to Tankerton Street, and Mary Ann said to James Ansell, 'If I was you, Father, I would not let them have a postmordal [sic] examination.' He said, deferring to her education and employment, 'Well, if you think so, sit down and write a few lines.' She did exactly that, addressing Dr Case, Dr Elkins' predecessor, attacking with a striking rhetorical question, 'For why do you want a postmordal examination on the body after being under your care for 4 years we decline to give you authority to hold one I remain Yours Mr Ansell.'

We hear the authentic tone of Mary Ann Ansell: shrill, querulous, parrying, not particularly respectful of authority. It is the voice of the rising underdog, endowed by the Board School movement, just as the anti-educationists had feared, had predicted anarchy. The doctors were not prepared to leave it at that, and there was another route – the coroner's power. Dr Elkins communicated with the Watford coroner, Mr TJ Broad, who ordered an immediate post-mortem. A serious enquiry had been set in motion, and there was no question of a death certificate.

On March 17th, watched closely by Dr Elkins, Dr Alfred Cox examined the body of Caroline Ansell and found that she had been a well-nourished young woman. There were no marks of violence. There were signs which led him to believe that death had occurred from acute irritant poisoning. Although he could find no evidence of poison in the viscera, he had very little doubt that the poison was phosphorus. He removed all the viscera for analysis and their appearance was compatible with irritant poisoning. He handed the jars, with a soiled sheet and another piece of linen, later found to be a portion of a nightdress stained with vomited blood, to the police. Detective Superintendent William Wood, stationed at Watford, was instructed to take charge of the case and gather information for an inquest. With a small team of two detectives he soon entered the asylum and began to question all the staff and inmates affected, down to the postal officer who delivered the two anonymous parcels. The cake was obviously the centre-piece of the mystery, but not a crumb of it remained. Wood had hopes that a search might turn up the brown paper wrapper. The wrapper for the tea and sugar parcel must have been viewed as lost beyond recall: it was given no prominence. Both the parcels had been addressed specifically to Caroline Ansell and found their target: no maniac had been distributing poison randomly. Christiana Edmunds, still in Broadmoor in 1899, had scattered poisoned chocolates around the shops of Brighton for her own ends, in the cause of frustrated love, without caring whom they harmed. That is not to say that the person who sent the cake took any account of the likelihood that the delicacy might be shared with others. Someone who knew Caroline must have intended to kill her – so the reasoning went – but she had been shut away, out of circulation, for nearly five years. It was incalculable. Theoretically, perhaps, a fellow inmate might have borne a grudge, as happens in places of confinement. A discharged person – some were discharged – could have done it, but it was far-fetched. A truly insane man or woman could have wished to eliminate Caroline for some irrational reason, but that, too, was far-fetched. She was an inconspicuous, harmless 'imbecile', lost in the maw of the great asylum. Was there any history or drama from the past?

The superintendent moved to the other sphere of enquiry – the dead girl's home environment. Harriett Parish was interviewed, but, fortunately for her, was not seen as a suspect: she could have had a bad time. On March 17th, Sergeant Stoten was despatched to 1 Tankerton Street, where the father handed over the false 'Harriett Parish' letter; Caroline's pathetic letter home in reply; and her further letter when she knew that her parents lived. On that same day, Wood sought out Mary Ann and questioned her generally: she was not at all reticent about her part in the letter from her father which sought to countermand a post-mortem. It is very likely that the superintendent's suspicions about her were crystallizing at this time. He carried on, with his men, preparing for the inquest, which was opened next day, on Saturday afternoon, March 18th, in the unlikely setting of the asylum recreation hall. The Coroner, Mr TJ Broad, sat with a jury of thirteen. In his opening address to the jury, he remarked that it appeared clear to him from what he had been told that death was due in a measure to an irritant poison, and how the deceased got that except from this portion of cake which she ate of course could not be ascertained. Still, there were various other things in connection with this case which perhaps it was unnecessary now for him to mention. An adjournment might be necessary.

Nurse Felmingham was the chief witness, since she had been present on the ward during the events which had led to a death. Her position was slightly delicate, although she was not criticised in court, because she was the intermediary who had unknowingly delivered the agent of death into the victim's hands. Although not to blame, perhaps in dark moments she wished that she had acted differently *at some stage*. Now that she was to be called to court a number of times, an ordeal for an obscure young woman in a hard and disregarded job, her recollection of the exact nature of the cake tended to vary. As in all the asylums, the ratio of attendant to inmate was lamentably low.[12] In the case of 'imbeciles', especially,

---

12 Monica Diplock (op cit, p. 22) describes staff problems around 1898: 'Many attendants were leaving after short periods, some to go to County Asylums where the rate of pay was higher. Reasons given for not wishing to stay included the requirement to perform menial tasks not considered to be "nursing", especially (I) standing in cold corridors

there was an expectation that they could be managed well enough on a shoestring – for that was what it was – with the aid of a strict routine. Epileptics surely required extra staff. Two on ward with a supervisor on call seems unreasonable.

Family members were present at the inquest, their fares surely paid for. Mary Ann Ansell was not listed to be called, but Superintendent Wood and Sergeant Peck had an informal 'conversation' with her, in the corridor, as it were, during which she said that she and Caroline never had been friends. Later, she denied those words. The mother, Sarah, told the coroner that she herself could not read or write. She had not sent a present of any kind to Caroline since Christmas twelve month, because she was too poor. Nor could she suggest anyone else who might have sent her presents: 'No, they are all as bad off as myself.' She knew nothing about any cake. Bewildered, out of her depth, plucked from a bare place of poverty, she cut a sad figure, but still managed to speak up. As proceedings continued, however, on later occasions, all concerned were to see her lose control and disintegrate.

Harriett Parish, too, was brought in from the slums formally to attest to her lack of any involvement in the happenings. She said that she had never sent anything to Caroline. Only one lawyer was in court – Mr Rowland Beevor, of the firm of Williams and James, representing the Metropolitan Asylums Board. An apparent poisoning had occurred while the victim was in the care of the board. No censure was, however, to be levelled at the asylum and its staff. The full, regulated procedure for the reception of parcels had been adhered to, and the disaster could not have been anticipated. No doubt even more rules were introduced thereafter.

Nurse Felmingham had personally handed to Superintendent Wood on his visit to the asylum a Christmas card sent to Caroline by Mary Ann Ansell, signing herself POLLIE. This was now before the

---

whilst the patients clean them, for two hours each morning; (II) going with the trolleys and distributing the food, clean clothes etc; (III) continual changing from ward to ward. On account of the small staff, a nurse is sometimes in two or three wards a day.' They also complained of the '"dullness of living in the country and distance from railway station"'.

coroner. The nurse stated that in her opinion the handwriting on the cake parcel was like that on the Christmas card and the false Harriett Parish letter. This was obviously very important evidence and the foreman of the jury immediately asked the pertinent question: 'Was the wrapper on the parcel destroyed?' The superintendent spoke up: 'We have had a good search, but cannot find it.'

Mary Driscoll, a lucky cake eater, looking weak and ill, was coaxed into court to tell her tale. She was the only stricken Leavesden inmate judged by the doctors to be mentally competent to give evidence. All that night she said, she had felt very bad and vomited very much. She was bad the next day, too. The bitter taste had lasted until the following Wednesday. Dr Blair was there to recount the events, but could not take the evidence any further forward. Dr Cox recorded his finding of the appearances of irritant poisoning. The afternoon had worn on, and the coroner adjourned the inquest pending an expert's analysis of the contents of the stomach. James Ansell and Mary Ann Ansell had not yet been called, it was noted.

Superintendent Wood had three weeks in which to pursue further enquiries. He was particularly anxious to find the brown paper wrapping. At first he had gathered that it had been destroyed with the general refuse, but a new, all-out search succeeded when, on Monday, March 20th, Police Sergeant Stoten and Police Constable Pigott discovered it in a heap of unspecified rubbish in the airing-court on the female side of the asylum. This was a turning-point in the investigation. The paper still bore the handwriting of the sender, stamps to the value of two pence and a postmark from WC – i.e. Bloomsbury.

On April 6th, Superintendent Wood made a move. He called at 42 Great Coram Street, where Mary Ann Ansell was at her place of work, and arrested her. He had two detectives with him. He read the arrest warrant over to her and administered the caution. 'I know nothing about it,' she said. 'I AM AS INNOCENT A GIRL AS EVER WAS BORN.' She spoke like a character in a novelette. Wood pressed on: 'What have you got in your pocket?' 'Only this paper,' she said, and handed him a piece of blue paper on which she had written some questions which she was intending to ask in person at the resumed inquest. It was a remarkable feat of preparation for someone in her station of life. The hectoring style resembles her letter for her father, refusing the post-mortem. It was a series of rhetorical questions – her favourite combative device:

> Why was we not sent for to see my sister before she was near death so we could have a word with [her] in time to see who it was that had been sending the parcel to her.
>
> When the nurse that was suppose to examine the cake found it was heavy why did she not make a further examinem on it and when one of the inmates was seen to spit it and why was the others allowed to finish eating it When friends are sent for to come and see the inmates either in life or death is it a rule that when an attendant take you to the place where the body is to be viewed for you to shut the door in your face and tell you to wait there until it thinks it proper for to allow you to go and view that what you are looking for and is it another rule that a body to lay some days before the face is wash and to fetch friends for about 26 miles to see the body and then to find it in a dirty condition when in such places are suppose to be so clean.
>
> When Caroline Ansell was placed under the care of a doctor and nurse and put in the infirmary what was she put in there for was it for sickness or Poison Poison [sic] if they had any idea of that she was suffering from any unsuspected complaint why did they not send word to her parents in good time if that had been done this trouble would not have happened.

It was all very well for the *London Daily News* (April 11th, 1899) which had been so admirably scrupulous in rendering an exact copy (in print) of the 'blue paper' to comment that, 'The writing was that of an apparently very indifferently educated person, bad in form, and, as will be seen, inaccurate in spelling', when the marvel is that such a girl – first generation in her family – had so adequate a vocabulary and the mental skill to marshal some rather sharp criticisms of the asylum. She was blaming Leavesden for the tragedy, and in that way it was clever as it seems like the genuine outburst of a bereaved person looking for someone to blame. There is the sarcasm of the barrack-room lawyer.

If we compare this astonishing tirade with Mary Ann's other known writings, it is written more carefully and legibly, perhaps as if copied, tongue between teeth. We can see a better syntax, a more assured vocabulary, and above all, an improved flow of thought. It is suggested that a person of superior intelligence but of 'indifferent' education, not the Molonys, who were of good education, a friend, a crony, has sat down with her and helped her to formulate the points, and that she has copied it out, possibly from a draft. Little enough at the time was made of the blue paper, but it told against her when all her activities were computed together. Nothing incriminating was found in the kitchen, and Superintendent Wood took his prisoner away to Watford Police Station, where she appeared that evening, before Mr Watkins, JP, and was remanded in custody to the Petty Sessions.

The arrest of the dead girl's own sister half-way through the inquest proceedings caused a sensation. National newspapers had caught up with the case. *Lloyd's Weekly*, published the day before the resumed inquest, somewhat pre-empted matters by saying that, 'It is also stated that Mary Ann Ansell purchased at different times five bottles of James' phosphor paste, presumably for the purpose of poisoning rats, from an oil-shop next door to 42 Great Coram Street.' The reporter had been extremely active in the neighbourhood: he had also secured an interview with Mrs Margaret Molony who gave him the first of a series of increasingly patterned summations of Mary Ann's character: she did her work very well, and was fairly well-behaved. SHE WAS ABOUT TO BE MARRIED. After the boarders left the house, at ten o'clock in the morning, there was nobody in except Ansell and herself and the two children. Ansell had plenty of time when she (the landlady) and her children were out, to make and bake a cake, but she never saw her servant baking, nor did she ever authorise her to buy phosphor paste.

For good measure, *Lloyd's Weekly* featured a drawing of the prisoner in court on remand, flanked by a policeman, and this early likeness was the inspiration for future illustration. It showed a dark, tousled young woman with heavy features, a large chin, and an expression which may be interpreted as sullen, defiant, or simply incredulous. She was wearing a treasured short cloak. The *Royston*

Crow - Herts and Cambs Reporter remarked that, 'The prisoner is not an unattractive young woman, and seems to have held a good situation.' Both comments are coloured to make Mary Ann appear more interesting and appealing.

Locally, the *St Albans Gazette* (March 29th, 1899) had reported cautiously:

> Another member of the family has been subpoenaed to attend on April 10th. This is deceased's sister, Mary Ann Ansell. She is a girl in service in Bloomsbury, and her mistress, with whom she has been for a long time, gives her an excellent character, and what light she can be expected to throw on the mystery it is not easy to conceive. At all events, never did the police have a more hopeful chance of solving a mystery. The crime appears to be the work of somebody who is ignorant as well as criminal; and to believe that a fugitive of this kind can long baffle the police, aided as the latter are by the strongest clue they could desire in the possession of the all-important wrapper, would surely be to underestimate the capacities of the force for investigation.

The *Daily Mail* sent a reporter to 42 Great Coram Street, where this time Mr Molony was happy to be interviewed, and he spoke out quite freely. His memory was not so good as his wife's: he thought that Mary Ann had been with them for only two and a half years. They were greatly surprised when she was arrested. He said, and the reporter eagerly picked up the crucial information, not previously brought out, that Mary was *'of very limited intelligence.'* She had never done anything to lead them to suspect that she had anything to do with the murder of her sister. She had shown no malice towards her and when she heard of her death, she wept bitterly, and seemed genuinely grieved. Some years ago, they had used phosphorus paste to kill rats. They had not authorised Mary Ann to get poison.

The recreation room was crammed with newspaper represent-atives on April 10th at about 3 pm when the inquest was re-opened. Mary Ann was not going to be present at all. She had previously been brought up and charged and therefore the subpoena was no longer applicable. She remained in custody, while several of her family had turned up. The enquiry was now directed *ad personam* – Mary Ann Ansell. All present knew that she was a suspect. There was a different, sharper atmosphere – not a woolly apprehension that a mystery was afoot. Mr CE Longmore, the County Solicitor, appeared for the police, and Mr R Beevor watched for the Board again. No one was there for Mary Ann. The jury elected a new foreman, the previous one submitting a medical certificate.

There was a great deal of new and substantial evidence. In particular, the testimony of Mr John Cooper caused a stir in court, because it pointed to a motive where none previously had been imaginable. He stated that he was agent for the Royal London Friendly Society, 16 Parliament Street, Finsbury. As a collector of insurance money, one of his duties was to call at 42 Great Coram Street, and he was acquainted with the sole servant there, Mary Ann Ansell, who sometimes gave him Mr Molony's regular payments. From time to time, up to September, he used to ask Miss Ansell if she would like to insure herself. She said that she might do so, later on. As she was paying him her master's premiums on September 6th, 1898, she told him that she would like to insure her sister's life. This information caused a sensation in court.

Cooper continued when the room was quiet again. Miss Ansell said that she and her sister, Caroline, were very fond of each other, and, in the event of anything happening, she would like to be able to bury her respectably. She said that her sister lived at Watford and was a general servant at the asylum. If his office had known that she was in fact a lunatic there, they would not have insured her life. He asked about Caroline's health, and she replied, 'She is as healthy, or healthier, than I am.' He told her the terms: a premium of 3d per week would provide £22 10s full benefit, which would be her entitlement. However, the insured person had to stay alive for six months before insurance could be paid out, and then the money due was only half benefit. Therefore, Mary Ann would have been entitled to half benefit of £11 5s on March 6th, 1899, provided that Caroline Ansell died of natural causes. In fact, she was to die on March 14th. Mary Ann began to pay out at the rate of 1s per month, and her final payment was on February 20th.

By the last post on the evening of March 17th, he, John Cooper, received a letter from Mary Ann, couched in correct Board School form for a business transaction:

> Dear Mr Cooper I send these few lines to ask your advice what I should do about my sisters insurance as she died on Tuesday and can you come and see me tomorrow as early as possible If you can call I would be very grateful as I don't know what to do about the three weeks arrears
>
> I remain
Yours truly
Miss Ansell

In fact there were no arrears. Mary Ann was confused about the situation. John Cooper was unable to call, but he replied by letter, instructing her to take the death certificate (which had not, in fact, been issued) together with the policy, to the nearest branch of the company, where she would be paid the sum due. When, however, he read in the newspaper that Caroline Ansell, a lunatic, and an inmate, not a servant, had died at the asylum of suspected poison, he was very worried. He went to 42 Great Coram Street on March 20th, and informed Miss Ansell that she had made a false statement, so that the company would not entertain her claim. She said that she was very sorry, but did not know the difference at the time. She hoped that he would not get into trouble. He told her that if she would hand over the policy and the premium book, he would get the premiums returned to her, but she said that she could not find them – she had mislaid them. He asked her if she had already been for the money, and she said that she had not done so, as she was to wait for the inquest.

The court digested this enlightening evidence, and then a juror asked, 'Is it possible to insure another person without his or her knowledge?' 'Yes, in the case of a relative.' Juror: 'I never knew that before.' Mr Longmore made a contribution which was found amusing: 'The Queen is insured by hundreds of people and never knows it.'

Mrs Margaret Molony's position, when she was called, was slightly awkward, just as Nurse Felmingham's had been. She knew that it was thought that the lethal cake had been baked in her own kitchen. Perhaps in some part of her mind she thought that she should have known about it, prevented the catastrophe. Mary Ansell, she had been told, was saying that she had been sent out by her for rat poison, and she was determined to refute that idea. Now she absolutely denied having sent her out on such an errand, even to destroy rats.

Equally worrying, she had liked the girl well enough, and trusted her around the two young children. She knew the other Ansell children too. She had been aware that Mary Ann had insured her sister in the London Friendly Society: the girl had told her that she would not present her claim until after the inquest, and mentioned that she had accidentally burnt the insurance policy. Mrs Molony had said that she had been very foolish, but that she thought that the company would pay out. The coroner wanted more specificity about the rats. There were some in the house, occasionally, and she (Mrs Molony) used to set traps for them. She did her own cooking, but Mary Ann had the opportunity to use the range when she was out, although she had never known her to do so.

The police had easily traced a likely source of the phosphorus early on in the investigation. Just around the corner from Great Coram Street at 43 Marchmont Street, there was an oil and colourman – a kind of general chandler, useful in that crowded neighbourhood. They certainly sold poisons. Emily Noakes was now brought to say that Mary Ann Ansell constantly came into her father's shop. About one month ago, she had asked for some phosphor paste, as they had a great many rats, and she had been supplied with four or five bottles since January 1st. Each cost 1d.

Dr Thomas Stevenson, of Guy's Hospital, Senior Scientific Advisor to the Home Office, was the eminent expert whose analysis had held back the resumption of the inquest. The court listened closely as he described his examination of the parts which he had received from Detective Superintendent Wood: the tongue, the vocal organs, part of the gullet, the kidneys, liver, gall bladder, spleen, stomach, and other organs of the deceased girl. The condition was characteristic of phosphorus poisoning, which produced fatty degeneration of the liver, kidneys and heart within two or three days of its administration, together with haemorrhages, which he had indeed noticed. *He had searched especially for traces of phosphorus with negative results,* but that was quite consistent with death from that cause, phosphorus being rarely detected when the patient survived three or four days after it had been given. He had seen the same results in cases where it was known that phosphorus had been taken. Having read the depositions from the previous hearing he was of the opinion that the symptoms shown by the deceased woman were those of phosphorus poisoning, and that this was the cause of death.

A juror pressed for more information, and Dr Stevenson said that he thought that the case was hopeless when seen by doctors. The symptoms would not appear for a day or two, and then it would be too late to save life. If the deceased had been treated for phosphorus poisoning immediately, she might have recovered, but the tendency was for symptoms to be of the slightest possible character at first. Dr Stevenson's evidence was not, on the whole, good news for the nursing staff at Leavesden, nor for the responsible head of that institution, Dr Elkins. Caroline had been kept on the ward in great pain with gross signs and symptoms for two whole days before Dr Blair was called. With hindsight, she was already dying when she first complained of biliousness and the whites of her eyes had turned yellow. Dr Stevenson's final point, that the initial symptoms are slight, was in the nurses' favour, since they could not reasonably have picked them up when Caroline was beginning to feel ill in bed overnight after eating the cake on the previous evening. Even so, some people, especially the jury, must have wondered if there might not have been a chance of recovery if medical help had been sought on that first morning. No doubt the nurses struggled with the timeless dilemma of not bothering Doctor. The asylum of 2000 souls was blessed with only two medical officers to patrol the many wards and manage the infirmary, while the medical superintendent himself, while not a stranger to those wards, spent much of his time in his office, swathed in red tape emanating from the Board, and engaged in what is now known as 'compliance'. Anyway, biliousness must have been taken more seriously there afterwards.

During the hiatus in the two afternoon hearings, Superintendent Wood had had time to brief a quasi-scientific witness, a recognised handwriting expert. This was Thomas Henry Gurrin, who said that he was used by Scotland Yard, the Bankers' Association and the Bank of England. That is, he commanded a fee which was his livelihood. He was, he deposed, strongly of the opinion that the 'Harriett Parish' letter, the Christmas card from 'Pollie', the blue paper, the brown wrapper and other documents in the case were all in the handwriting of Mary Ann Ansell. An attempt at disguise had been made on the cake wrapper, but it had not been skilfully executed, and the same applied to the 'Harriett Parish' letter. Thomas Gurrin was the last witness called by Mr Longmore. It was getting on for six o'clock in the evening as the coroner summed up, targeting Mary Ansell, naming her, as was admissible then, under the provisions of the Coroner's Act of 1887. That right was abolished much later, by the Act of 1988. He said that it was perfectly clear that the cake which the deceased received was poisoned, and Dr Stevenson was in no doubt that death was due to phosphorus. The wrapper went a long way to point to the sender. It was a curious thing that death should have occurred so soon after the six months' qualifying period for receiving the insurance pay-out. The jury had before them a witness who had sold bottles of poison to Mary Ann Ansell a month since: she said that it was for rats, but the girl's mistress said she was not much troubled with rats, and when she was, she set traps. Therefore, the girl lied to the shopkeeper. He hoped that the jury would not be influenced by anything that they had read in the press.

The jury retired for ten or fifteen minutes before returning their unanimous verdict:

> That Caroline Ansell died at Leavesden Asylum on the 14th of March, and her death was caused by eating a piece of cake on the 10th March containing phosphorus poisoning, such cake having been received by her through the post on the 9th March, and having been sent to her by her sister, Mary Ann Ansell, for the purpose of obtaining the insurance money payable under the life insurance policy on the life of Caroline Ansell.

Coroner: You find that Mary Ann Ansell has been guilty of wilful murder?

Foreman: Yes

Mr Longmore: On that, sir, I ask for a committal of the accused, now in custody at Watford. [Coroners' powers to commit a person for trial were to be lost by virtue of the Criminal Law Act, 1977.]

Coroner: Yes. Mary Ann Ansell stands committed to take her trial on the verdict of the Jury for wilful murder.

CHAPTER FOUR

THE COLOUR YELLOW

From now on, Mary Ann acquired a public presence as she was repeatedly brought into court from a dark cell and subjected to scrutiny. She will not have understood the sequence of the various hearings. Her demeanour and facial expressions were constantly commented on, and were an important factor in the way in which she was judged. Undoubtedly, her mood was at times misinterpreted. She was not clever enough, nor so advised, to compose her face into an appropriate and appealing mask. Bewildered, certainly, and defiant, a caged under-dog, she was seen as 'cold', 'collected', 'unconcerned', and, especially, 'sullen'. In fact she was recorded as being in tears, more often than people realised or admitted. At first, everyone wanted her to be a palpable monster.

The press had got their first sight of her, in the dock, with a policeman, before the magistrate on the evening of her arrest on April 6th. After the coroner's committal, she was put up again at the Watford police court on Tuesday, April 11th, but it was only a formal remand. The difference, this time, was that the roadway outside was lined by people who had failed to gain admission to the court. Mary Ann was faced with a full bench of magistrates, presided over by Mr JF Watkins, and a packed crowd of spectators. She knew Sergeant Stoten, who placed her in what on county court days served as the jury-box. She was charged that 'she did feloniously, wilfully, and of her malice aforethought kill and murder one Caroline Ansell, at Leavesden, Watford rural on the 14th day of March, 1899.'

There is a strong, if unkind description of the young prisoner:

> She wore a black hat, a jacket trimmed with cheap fur, and a dress which was considerably the worse for wear, her general appearance being that of a general servant in none too good circumstances. The prisoner had a somewhat sullen look, but hardly appeared to realise the gravity of her position. When her name was called she stepped almost jauntily to the front of the box. She had no solicitor, and looked straight towards the Bench with a curious air. (*Hemel Hempstead Gazette*, April 15th)

The *News of the World* of April 16th contributed detailed observations of the same type:

> She was not much to look at - a rather tall, commonplace girl, with bent shoulders and rough hands, a typical maid of all work: unattractive and untidy, features unlovely, complexion dull and pale, high cheekbones, sloping chin, lips red and protruding, expression stolid and sullen. She wore a crumpled skirt, a cape trimmed with fur, a black hat with spreading wings. If she felt any emotion she did not show it.

Superintendent Wood went into the witness box, and, after his previous evidence had been read over to him, asked for a further remand until the Thursday, when the Treasury would take up the prosecution. The Chairman agreed. Mary Ann was thought to be 'detached' again when she was brought up on the Thursday morning before the banque of five magistrates and the curious crowds. No doubt she was preoccupied by the severe toothache from which she had been suffering since being taken into custody, holding a handkerchief to her face.

The dental health of the poor was notoriously bad. Visits to a dentist were unaffordable. Only the better off used the toothbrushes and pastes which were certainly available. Weird and very expensive dentures, and 'stopping' were not an option for people like the Ansells. Decay and pain were an inevitable part of existence. Later that evening, in an act of humanity, the police surgeon, Dr GF Smith, was summoned to extract one of the prisoner's teeth. Then she was able to concentrate on what was happening to her.

This occasion, the actual full committal, was formal and very real, a step in a lethal pathway. The gravity of Mary Ann's situation was demonstrated by the presence of a new figure in court – her own solicitor, Mr Percy Wisbey, a local lawyer from Hemel Hempstead, in practice on his own account. He was astonishingly young, only twenty-two-years-old. Wheels had turned: the spectacle of a young woman of the poorest class standing alone on a capital charge was unacceptable. Legal aid had not yet been formulated. In 1903 and 1930, the Poor Prisoners' Defence Act, and later Legal Aid Acts from 1949, righted an obvious injustice. Some solicitors, before that relief, would appear *pro bono publico* but in this case it appears doubtful that young Mr Wisbey could afford such a gesture. He was having to earn a living. At least he would not have been expensive. Although, clearly, not a man of experience, he did prove competent to stand up and conduct the mini-trial into which committal had expanded. It was never revealed who actually paid Mary Ann's lawyers; the press, aware of the difficulty, made enquiries but could not isolate a donor, and suggested that friends had contributed. In fact, certain sympathisers who were beginning to surface, clergy, charities, her employers, as well as the Ansell clan with their pennies must have scraped together the bare minimum. It could be done.[13]

Mr Longmore, the County Solicitor, now prosecuted for the Treasury, not the police. He told the Bench that the father, James Ansell, had also taken out an insurance policy. It covered his own life and those of his wife and seven children, and the sum recoverable was £10, but it lapsed in February, 1899, because the premiums were in arrears. This information was included for completeness, and also because it showed that life insurance was a familiar issue in the Ansell family and not an isolated enterprise by Mary Ann.

During Mr C Elton Longmore's very accurate summary of the evidence against the accused, Percy Wisbey risked an interruption, springing up like a jack-in-a-box as he had learnt in small cases before

---

13 As an example, the impoverished father of the Boy Jones, Queen Victoria's stalker, managed to beg and borrow from his equally poor neighbours the astonishing sum of five guineas, in 1838, in order to pay for the services of 'the eloquent Mr William Prendergast, Barrister-at-Law', to save his son from prison or transportation. The Jones family, with their seven children, lived in one room, a hovel, in Bell Yard, Westminster, where they all slept on the floor, on miserable rags. See Jan Bondeson, *Queen Victoria's Stalker: The Strange Story of the Boy Jones*, p. 20.

the lower courts, to say of the blue paper that it was *not* admitted to be in his client's handwriting. The more experienced solicitor dealt with him smoothly, by explaining that he could understand in such a serious charge nothing would be admitted, but he understood that it was not disputed that the paper in question was in the prisoner's handwriting. He proceeded, without overvaluing Mr Gurrin's testimony, merely to state that he always thought that experts' evidence on handwriting was useful when pointing out the different forms in writing, and thus enabling the magistrates themselves to come to a conclusion as to whether or not incriminating documents were written by the accused person. He now put in the signature on the letter written for her by the Leavesden gate porter to add to the list of specimens written by Mary Ann Ansell.

In a case of poisoning, he said, 'one did not expect to find any direct evidence.' He would think that there had scarcely been a case where a person charged with poisoning had been seen actually to administer the substance. A chain of circumstantial evidence, sometimes strong, sometimes weak almost invariably lay behind a poisoning charge. It was now his painful duty to submit that the chain was irresistibly strong.

Mr Wisbey, rising, said that Mr Longmore had opened his case very fairly, but, as he himself had only been instructed the previous night, he would have to ask the Bench to allow him to reserve his cross-examination of the doctors until the adjournment. (He had, in fact, already seen his client, but only briefly, and not for long enough to take a proper statement. There was never any indication that he had a clerk to help him. He could see that the medical evidence was going to be crucial, and that he would have to undertake some research on poisons.) Consent was given, and the prosecution witnesses began to be called.

Nurse Alice Felmingham, back again, had her first taste of being cross-examined. Percy Wisbey was feeling his way; he elicited that the nurse did not remember what sort of wrapper was around the tea and sugar, nor what the writing on it was like. When Superintendent Wood was testifying, the solicitor did rather better by establishing that the superintendent had not cautioned Mary Ann Ansell before she made the damaging statement that she and Caroline never had been friends to him in his informal 'conversation' with her at the inquest, and Sergeant Peck had written it down. Wood explained that at the time he had been making general notes of the evidence to be produced at the enquiry by the several parties who had been summoned, among whom was Mary Ann Ansell: at that time there was no charge against Mary Ann. The court rose, and afterwards Percy Wisbey told a journalist that the defence would be a strict denial. So early, he had made up his mind. She had told him that she did not do it, and there it was. She came from a tough background where people did not plead guilty. There was always a chance that a jury would not convict. He would test the evidence and do his duty.

The court reconvened on Saturday morning, April 15th. Mary Ansell was looking better. She was allowed to sit, and 'appeared to regard the proceedings with complete indifference.' (*Lloyd's Weekly*, April 16th) Outside court, her mother had been waiting faithfully, and, even before the doors were opened, she had the first of her very public attacks of 'hysteria', in front of a large, gaping crowd. Not surprisingly, the Royal London Friendly Society had sent in counsel, Mr Geoghegan, with a watching brief, anxious that their practices might be impugned, their reputation tarnished.

The local medical man, Dr Cox, who had performed the post-mortem, was the first to face Percy Wisbey, who, it was apparent, had been studying medical texts, and was set on establishing that the death had been from natural causes – that the appearances of the body were similar to those of *acute yellow atrophy of the liver*, a perfectly proper line of defence employed in a long history of poisoning trials. He did rather well: Dr Cox allowed that there were similarities. This was only the committal, but Percy Wisbey was blazing the path for counsel to pursue at the trial which would undoubtedly take place.

Dr Stevenson was a formidable expert witness, used to argument with senior counsel, for a young solicitor to encounter in the police court. First, he supplied evidence about three bottles of phosphorus paste which Superintendent Wood had bought in Marchmont Street. They also contained starch paste, a little oil, and Prussian Blue (used for colouring). Each bottle held 4 grains of phosphorus – enough to kill three adults. (The lethal dose is 1 to 2 grains, with exceptions, according to *Taylor's Medical Jurisprudence*.) Cross-examined, he had to allow that no portion of the cake alleged to have been poisoned had been submitted to him for analysis. He was adamant that death was due to phosphorus poisoning. There were cases of phosphorus poisoning where the post-mortem appearances were very like those of acute atrophy of the liver. (The statement benefitted the prisoner only if you reversed the comparison.) Here the court adjourned for luncheon. On resumption, Mary Ann broke down and *cried bitterly*. Her eyes were red, but it was thought that she followed the evidence closely. From time to time, Percy Wisbey left his seat and consulted his client on some fresh point of evidence. She was especially interested in the handwriting, it was noted. Their professional relationship appeared to be satisfactory. The effect of these whispered consultations must have been that Mary Ann seemed to be fully competent to understand the flow of evidence and normal in her responses. With hindsight, the solicitor should have stayed in his place.

Dr Elkins made his first appearance in the witness-box. No one present would have known from his modest demeanour that he was, as it happened, an expert on phosphorus poisoning. He had seen the deceased, he testified, just before death, and the symptoms were consistent with that particular agent. The appearances at the post-mortem, where he assisted Dr Cox, were similar to those in another case of admitted phosphorus poisoning.

Nurse Felmingham and her colleague, Nurse Hussey, identified the cake wrapper, saying that they chiefly remembered it because the postage stamps were on the left-hand side, and one of them had remarked to the other, 'What a pity to waste two penny stamps on 2d worth of cake.' Harriett Parish was again obliged to deny that she had sent the false letter to Caroline, and she was not cross-examined.

James Ansell was a witness for the first time, and Percy Wisbey did cross-examine him, to his client's advantage. He said that Mary Ann and Caroline were friends, and he had never heard Mary Ann say a word against her sister. At home with his family, he called the false Harriett Parish letter his 'death warrant' a piece of wit which established his identity, however rough and illiterate he seemed in the court setting. Replying to Mr Wisbey, Miss Noakes, of Marchmont Street, said that she did not remember the prisoner's buying Keating's powder for beetles, thus frustrating an attempt to show that Mary Ann routinely bought poison for pests. Mrs Margaret Molony said that Mary Ann told her that she had accidentally burnt the insurance policy. She slept in the kitchen. She appeared to have everything that she wanted.

Suddenly, the case was over. The magistrates had devoted ten hours to the evidence. Mary Ann Ansell pleaded not guilty and reserved her defence. Committed for trial at the next Assizes, she was not entirely a lonely figure, because she had a solicitor who would stay with her and a family who would stand by her. They did not believe what was being said about her. All their concern was now bent on Mary Ann. Caroline had been lost to them already. They were realists in their very hard world: Caroline was off their hands, while her sister was lively, holding down a good job, earning money, a success, able to read and write, a valued presence. How could this have happened? They were appalled. There was an upsetting scene as Mary Ann was being led away to the police station, when her mother and a sister, who had been kept in one of the waiting rooms, met her in the corridor by chance, and she fell on them, crying, until the police managed to persuade her to leave the building.

As for Percy Wisbey, he had two and a half months in which to get up his case – a capital one, so early in his career – all on his own, while covering such other work, civil or criminal as came in. He had to instruct counsel, someone willing to appear for a reasonable fee, and write a brief which might or might not have included a full version of the fruits of his medical research. He might have left the bulk of that to his chosen barrister. He must have seen his incarcerated client, perhaps several times, and checked out her reaction to the prosecution points. He took a proof from her, that is, her statement of what had happened based on her adamant insistence that she was innocent. He had to think deeply about the consequences of the plea and how he was to run the case. He studied his law books. He was doing his best. What he should have done but did not, was to interview his client's connections, take proofs from them as potential witnesses on her behalf. If he had done so at that stage, the entire defence could have been different. It might have been that he saw it as an open-and-shut case, was afraid of stirring up a hornet's nest, and too inexperienced to contemplate a complex approach. He had counsel there to guide him, did he not? He probably travelled up to chambers in London for a conference.

There were weak points in the Treasury case – the circumstantial nature of it all, and, especially, the absence of poison in the viscera, and the similarity of the symptoms to disease or infection. That was the patent and indeed traditional route that the small defence team would pursue. The decision was made that Mary Ann Ansell should give evidence on her own behalf. The right of the accused to speak in the witness box was very new – provided by the Criminal Evidence Act, 1898, the previous year, and her lawyers were confident that she could perform well enough within the constraints of her background and education. In fact, she did not let them down, came up to proof, withstood a merciful cross-examination, and said nothing to embarrass them.

Percy Wisbey acted decisively when a gross contempt of court was published by the *Barnet and Finchley Herald*, to the effect that, '*Caroline did die, but Mary will never receive the gold pieces which were the price of her own sister's blood*'. He briefed Mr JR Randolph to take proceedings against the newspaper in the High Court, an expensive procedure, one would have thought, when funds were limited.

On the evening of Tuesday, 27th June, Mr Justice Mathew arrived by the 5.25 train at Hertford station and was met with conspicuous pomp by High Sheriff, Under Sheriff, and Sheriff's Chaplain, before being conveyed to the Judge's Lodgings at Hertford Castle gatehouse. An escort of mounted policemen, their horses burnished for the ceremonial duty, trotted with the carriage, forming a procession. The seated figure was to be the arbiter of Mary Ann's fate. The next morning, at 11 o'clock, the judge presided over the Grand Jury which opened the Summer Assizes at the Shire Hall, a commanding building, designed by James Adam. The Grand Jury was to be abolished in 1933, with exceptions, and entirely in 1948. Its function was to enquire into the evidence to see if was strong enough to return a 'true bill' for the accused to be indicted for trial, but it was already becoming a mere formality because the expanded committals were already covering the ground. It did provide a useful conspectus of the current crime scene, and the press was admitted.

His Lordship said that there was an unusually heavy calendar. The Jury of twenty-three gentlemen, with the local MP, Mr TF Halsey as foreman, were to hear fourteen cases, two of murder, two of attempted murder, and ten 'ordinary' but indictable crimes of arson, night poaching, embezzlement, assault, and attempted suicide.

The first of the two murders was agreed from the start to be a mad one. John Smith, aged 18, a labourer, had inflicted fifty wounds on Mercy Nicholls with his pocket-knife, and then marched along Railway Street like a sentry, shouting, 'Left, left, left! Let 'em come and I will give it to 'em!' Dr Boycott, Medical Superintendent of the new Hertfordshire County Asylum (Hill End), was called by the prosecution, with the agreement of the defence, to state that Smith was congenitally of weak mind, and of unsound mind at the time of the commission of the crime with delusions at that time. Two relatives had been in asylums (which were not specified) and there was inter-marriage between cousins. He was removed, via Hill End, to Broadmoor, to be detained until Her Majesty's pleasure was known. A reporter in court thought that he had a 'vacant' look as he was found unfit to plead by reason of insanity. The judge presided over all the arrangements in complete agreement with the outcome. The point is that the issue of insanity had been well prepared and was presented to the Court before the case was heard.

The Grand Jury had no difficulty in returning a true bill in the matter of the Ansell case and the trial was set to begin at the Shire Hall on the next day, Thursday, June 29th at 11 am. Mary Ann spoke up 'in a firm and determined voice' when she was called upon to state her plea, which was Not Guilty, as expected. She was wearing the same shabby clothes – a black hat and dress, with a fur-tipped cape. Well, of course she was, this was her habitual outfit, and no one was going to bring in a change of clothing for her as she waited in her spartan cell, used to hardship and discomfort. This was a girl with nothing except what she stood up in and one treasured necklace. She had no expectations of luxury or kindness. Compare her with Ruth Ellis, who was famously permitted to have her hair re-dyed platinum blonde in readiness for her murder trial, or Helen Snee, tried for conspiracy to commit murder at the Old Bailey in 1876, who had been snatched away from her home by the police when she was wearing 'an old dress, almost in rags' for her morning chores, and was allowed to receive more attractive clothes from her solicitor.

Counsel in court before His Honour Judge Mathew were Mr JP Rawlinson, QC and Mr Grubbe (a busy local barrister, always in court), who were prosecuting for the Treasury, and Mr William Clarke Hall and Mr Theobald Mathew for the defence. The factors, strands, relationships which influence the choice of the right barrister for the case can be complex, private, or even automatic when a solicitor regularly briefs a certain set of chambers. When the instructing solicitor settles a fee with the barristers' clerk, the eminence of the barrister, if available, and the solvency of the lay client are not the only deciding elements. We cannot know why Percy Wisbey came to William Clarke Hall for Mary Ann Ansell. He might have briefed him before. He would not have commanded a substantial fee. He was not eminent, not a silk.

Persuasively, perhaps, he was known to have charitable interests, and to have a background of helping under-privileged women and their children. Born in 1866, his father a clergyman, after Christ Church, Oxford, he was called to the bar (Gray's Inn) actually in 1899, according to *Who was Who*. His special interest, on which he published, was the law relating to children. Early on, he had encountered Benjamin Waugh, a Non Conformist Minister, founder, in 1887, of the NSPCC. He was captivated by Waugh's beautiful daughter, Edna, a promising artist, and encouraged her to attend the Slade, under Sir Henry Tonks. He himself was short and fair-haired. In 1899, the year of the Ansell trial, when he was thirty-three years old, he married Edna, but there was tumult and ambivalence virtually from the start. The emotional disaster is well evidenced by Edna's diaries and documented in biographies.

There is no getting away from it, 'Willie' was one of the not-unknown species of husbands who are philanthropic in their public persona, and bullies and tyrants at home. He was neglectful, returning from Gray's Inn to his country home at the weekends with an orphan in tow, sometimes leaving the child with Edna. 'O why does a man engrose (*sic*) his mind in this cause of prostitutes leaving his wife sick to the heart in loneliness,' she wrote. Even more to his discredit, Clarke Hall abandoned his praise of Edna's art, disliking her spontaneity and wanting her to produce heavy oils, thus nearly destroying her creative powers. His rejection of the artist in Edna was total. He did not want to see her work around their home, Red Cottage. One day he asked her to remove her drawings from the dining-room walls. If he went home and found signs of her art, he would demand angrily, 'What is all this rubbish lying around?' This was the private life of the lawyer deputed to try to save Mary Ann from the gallows. In the future, he was to have children of his own and to be devoted to the work of the NSPCC and highly influential in that cause.

The Right Honourable John Frederick Peel Rawlinson QC[14] opened the case for the Crown. Coming to the false 'Harriett Parish' letter, received by Caroline on March 24th, he now gave an explanation for its purpose, which, until this occasion, had been obscure. He put it to the jury that, by the rules of the Asylum, if an inmate were taken

---

14 An Establishment figure, eminent lawyer, Inner Temple, Eton, Trinity College, Cambridge. Took silk 1897. Vice chairman of the Bar, etc. See *Dictionary of National Biography*.

seriously ill, notice was at once sent to the relatives, and further notice was sent if death resulted. The person who sent the letter knew that if poison in the tea and sugar had been ingested on the 22nd or 23rd of the month and caused illness, the Asylum authorities would write at once to the parents and an inquiry might be raised. The false letter was sent, counsel suggested, for the purpose of leading the Asylum officials to think that it was *of no use to send a report to the parents, because they were dead.* Counsel's explanation made perfect sense and, of course, was damaging to Mary Ann. He also pointed out that 'the prisoner was in near communication with the family at home, and would probably be acquainted with what had occurred'. (His meaning was that when she found out that the first attempt to poison had failed, she went out and bought more of the same.)

Clarke Hall cross-examined most of the Crown witnesses. Nurse Alice Felmingham was brought to say that there had been a great deal of illness at the Asylum during the last three weeks.

Counsel: Does this paragraph in the newspaper accurately describe the state of things?: "About fifty of the patients of the Leavesden Asylum under the Metropolitan Asylums Board are suffering from a mysterious disease which is believed to be enteritis or typhoid."?

Felmingham: I don't know about that, because the patients are isolated.

Judge: Do you know what the nature of the disease is?

Felmingham: I heard it was typhoid.

Clarke Hall: You have heard that there was a good deal of mystery connected with it?

Felmingham (pluckily): I don't think I said that.

The foreman of the jury was curious about the sugar sent with the tea and presumed to have been poisoned. Had the nurse noticed anything unusual about it? This was just the sort of question that Mr A MacPherson, who was holding a watching brief for the Asylums Board, was there to take special note of, but she was equal to it: since the substance was ordinary demerera, if any yellow substance had been mixed with it, she really did not notice it.

Both the Ansell parents were pressed into court again, for the Crown, an unhappy situation, but there was opportunity for cross-examination favourable to their daughter. They could see her, watching from the dock. Clarke Hall got James to say what he had always said, that Mary Ann and Caroline were on good terms. He had no reason to think that Mary (as he called her) was in distress for money. Sarah Ansell was sure that the two sisters were happy and comfortable together, and she had never heard a bad word said about either of them.

Mrs Molony's evidence was not entirely willing. She told Clarke Hall that Mary Ann had plenty of clothes, and she knew of no reason why the girl should want money. Mr Rawlinson re-examined. He knew that Mrs Molony had stated previously that there was an expectation of marriage, and now he was going to bring it out, because it strengthened the already well established financial motive for murder. 'No reason?' he asked, and Mrs Molony had to answer. 'She anticipated marriage.' When was that? 'It was expected to take place at Easter, but it was postponed to Whitsuntide.' Why was that? *She did not tell me why.*

Evidentially, the fiancé should have been in court, subpoenaed, but he was an invisible man. He seemed to have gone to ground, perhaps afraid of being suspected as an accomplice, but surely Superintendent Wood would have searched and found him, with his usual diligence. His name was never uttered. Possibly Mr X was a man of bad character, and the superintendent had warned the prosecution about him, so that they did not *want* to call him. Mrs Molony would have known his name, where he lived, surely, since he was a 'follower', allowed, within reason, to frequent her kitchen. She certainly knew more than she was saying, and courteous Mr Rawlinson chose not to press her further.

The Crown attached great importance to handwriting evidence, to the effect that all the relevant exhibits were in the prisoner's hand. Although there were some critics, graphology was widely regarded as a valuable discipline, with its opinions admissible in court. Thomas

Henry Gurrin, of 59 Holborn Viaduct, was the acknowledged expert in dozens of cases and very capable of standing up for himself when challenged, as here, to admit that he could not always be right. In the Adolph Beck case of 1896, three years before *Ansell*, a notorious miscarriage of justice, based on mistaken identification evidence, Gurrin had substantially contributed to the wrong conviction of Beck. Now, in 1899, when Beck was serving his first sentence of penal servitude, there was doubt about his guilt, and, of course, the Home Office knew so, but the Crown was still happy to employ Gurrin. It was not until 1904 that Gurrin unreservedly withdrew his opinion that Beck's handwriting was that of the real swindler, namely John Smith (really Weiss), and Beck was accorded a Free Pardon.

The Court listened solemnly as Clarke Hall approached Gurrin's very decided and definitive pronouncements. The expert agreed that the writing-paper referred to was no doubt very common. The character of the writing of a person frequently writing, he said, was more marked than that of a person who did not write much. There were two sorts of 'o's' in one letter, and two different 's's' in another, but that was quite common in the same document. The word 'Asylum' was incorrectly spelt on one document (the blue paper) that was admitted, but on the cake wrapper it was spelt correctly. He had pointed that out at the police court, rather as favourable to the accused. Writing on brown paper would modify the handwriting somewhat. One dubious point on which Counsel had not made any demur was that, in describing the similarity between the 'Harriett Parish' letter and that by Mary Ann Ansell to the insurance agent, they each begin with the same words: 'I now send these few lines.' It is obvious if we set these two letters against the two written by Caroline Ansell that all the Board School pupils used the same stereotypical formulae. Possibly Clarke Hall did not recognise that. Mr Gurrin agreed that, while it was indeed true that uneducated persons wrote the same class of handwriting, they did not have the same characteristics.

When it came to the copious medical evidence, the main sphere of Clarke Hall's lucubrations, this was where the standard of his cross-examination picked up, as he tried to raise doubt that the cause of death was, in fact, phosphorus poisoning. He was chasing the phantom of the disease of yellow atrophy, handicapped by the fact that the liver here was not atrophied. To that end, he had found a helpful medical authority, Dr Wickham Legg (1843–1921), physician at St Bartholomew's, once medical attendant to Prince Leopold, Queen Victoria's haemophiliac son, lecturer and author of many published papers, whom he quoted as saying that it was possible for the liver under acute yellow atrophy to be of normal or even enlarged size.

There was going to be no consensus here. Dr Thomas Stevenson absolutely refuted Dr Wickham Legg's opinion, and the latter was not called by the defence.

Dr Stevenson insisted that, from the post-mortem, there were no symptoms at all of yellow atrophy, which was a very rare disease. He had experienced only two cases in more than thirty years. Moreover, he stated, several well known authorities held that yellow atrophy was actually a form of phosphorus poisoning! The symptoms described by the medical witnesses were entirely those of phosphorus poisoning. He did not find the actual presence of phosphorus in the body, and did not expect to do so. Asked about the bitter tea and sugar, he thought that phosphorus could not very well be introduced by that means without being noticed.

The weak point about the 'yellow atrophy' defence was that other sufferers had eaten the cake, and one had nearly died. Mr Rawlinson re-examined Dr Stevenson, who said that he had never heard of two such cases (of yellow atrophy) occurring in an institution. Two cases at the same time would be extraordinary, and three cases even more so. Dr Cox was no more amenable to the defence: at post-mortem, he too found the liver to be of normal size, with no signs of atrophy. Asked now to state the difference between phosphorus poisoning and yellow atrophy, he said that the difference was in size.

Clarke Hall had another string to his bow. Asylums were known to be prone to epidemics, and he was going to try to raise the doubt that Caroline Ansell might have died from enteritis or typhoid. An outbreak of infectious enteric disease was much more credible than a mass outbreak of yellow atrophy. He had elicited from Nurse Felmingham a history of typhoid at Leavesden, but it was recent, after the decease of Caroline Ansell, and, although quite helpful, showing that the asylum was not immune from epidemics, obviously a previous sickness would have been more valuable.

The Crown was well aware that this line of inquiry would be pursued by the defence, and a negation was brought out in Dr Elkins' examination-in-chief, when he stated that during the months of January, February and March, of 1899 there had been no trouble in the asylum in the nature of zymotic diseases (ie, nothing epidemic, endemic, contagious or sporadic). Since April, there had been an outbreak of enteritis and typhoid. There were some symptoms in enteritis and typhoid similar to those which had been described, *but typhoid was a much longer disease.* Dr Elkins' evidence had drawn the teeth of Clarke Hall's cross-examination, but he struggled on. Since typhoid had been more or less destroyed, ruled out, by Elkins, counsel's preferred notional disease was now the vaguer, less closed, condition of enteritis. Asked to clarify, the doctor said that there were some fifty patients suffering from either typhoid or enteritis: enteritis might be produced by poisons of various kinds.

Discretely keeping his testimony to the minimum, not tempted towards expansion, he did not reveal that he had first-hand experience of phosphorus poisoning. He had contributed an admirable study of a case of suicide by that means to the *British Medical Journal* of December 19th, 1891. A depressed female patient, not certified, kept in a private asylum, confessed that she had sucked and chewed the phosphorus ends of two boxes of red-headed matches, 'Cleopatra Needle Matches, Bryant and May'. Her consequent vomit was not kept, and apparently did not attract attention by luminosity or odour. (Those well-known characteristics, with the odour being that of garlic, were not featured in the Ansell trial.) Her illness was short, mild at first. Jaundice appeared, and the liver became painful. The heart began to fail. She had a great thirst, was delirious, kept saying 'yellow'. Wild movements came on. There was an expression of pain, but more often of intense mania. The eyes stared, the eyebrows were elevated, the teeth clenched, and the pupils fully dilated. Death came about one hundred hours after taking the poison. 'For the sum of two-thirds of a penny this poor lady accomplished her end.' The pathologist found that the liver was of a very pale canary yellow colour. The pathological interest of the case lay in changes in the nerve cells of the cortex.

In court, in 1899, Dr Blair, who had cared for the dying patient, gave Clarke Hall no trouble. So far as he knew, he said cautiously, all the symptoms in the illness of Caroline Ansell were similar to those of acute yellow atrophy. (We should remember here that he is referring only to symptoms, not to post mortem changes, because he did not attend the autopsy.) He did not know that yellow atrophy was hastened by irritant poisons. Poison which caused enteritis might indeed be taken by various people with different effects. Clarke Hall asked, 'All the people in the Asylum might have taken the same kind of poison, and only these fifty have been affected?' To this weird, fanciful question, Dr Blair could only reply with a short affirmative. Clarke Hall was proposing a desperate remedy for the overdose of stricken cake eaters. It is fair to say that he had sown confusion around the medical evidence. That was the time when he was most on his feet, and he made the scientific element of the trial more mysterious and important than it really was. Yellow atrophy washed over the minds of the tired-out jury.

The long court day was over, the prosecution case exhausted. Clarke Hall let it be known that he would be calling the defendant herself next morning. The jury were marshalled off, doomed to sleep uncomfortably in the Assembly Room at the Shire Hall, their only consolation a country drive in the evening to the village of Watton-at-Stone and back.

CHAPTER FIVE

'AND WRETCHES HANG THAT JURYMEN MAY DINE'

On Friday, July 30th, 1899, the second and final day of the trial, at 10.30 am, Clarke Hall put his client in the witness box, and the crowded court stilled. Would she be incoherent, inaudible, too overawed to stand up for herself – a poor, trembling servant told off by her master in the largest of halls imaginable, stared at by disapproving faces? Not a bit of it. Mary Ann Ansell was stolidly ready to answer her counsel's plain questions. She was twenty-two years of age, she did write the letter refusing the post-mortem, at her father's dictation, but she knew nothing about the letter signed Harriett Parish, nor the brown paper wrapper. It was true that she had, on four or five occasions, bought phosphor paste from Mr Noakes' shop – the shop where she always bought things for her employers. The first time was in January. She needed the paste for the rats in the basement kitchen. They had annoyed her. She did not tell her mistress that she had bought the poison. She had told Mrs Molony about the rats, but no notice was taken. That was why she bought the poison for her own protection, because she was frightened. She did not remember saying to Superintendent Wood that she was not friends with Caroline, for *'Two better sisters there never was than me and my sister what is dead.'*

It was true that she did insure Caroline's life, and it was no secret to anybody. She told her mistress directly she had done it. Her wage was £13 per year and she was never in great want of money or clothing between September, 1989 and March, 1899. She had plenty of everything. She did not send the cake or the tea and sugar. (She was asked if she had *made* the cake and denied it.) She had sent nothing to her sister except a letter in December. She had no knowledge of sending the Christmas card which contained her writing. It must have been sent three or four Christmases before.

Cross-examined, not harshly, by Mr Rawlinson, she acknowledged the letters to the insurance agent and the registrar as being in her handwriting. She bought the paper in Marchmont Street, not as a packet, but a pennyworth loose, at the shop she generally went to. She put the phosphorus poison down a rat hole. She pushed it in with a stick and did not spread it on anything.

'Did you ever succeed in killing any rats with this poison?'

'No, only I smelt a peculiar smell as if some of the rats had died from the effects.' (This exchange is not verbatim. The journalist has pruned Mary Ann's answers into decent English, which gave a false impression of her capability to contemporary readers.)

'Do you mean to tell the jury that dead rats were lying about under the kitchen without your mistress knowing about it?'

'She had smelt them on one occasion.'

'How many rat holes were there?'

'They were all over the place.'

'Did you show them to your mistress?'

'She knew of them.'

'How about the burning of the policy and the book? When did that take place?'

'After Mr Cooper had called. He asked for the policy and I had not time to look for it. Afterwards it got amongst some other papers that I burnt, and I did not see the book until it was too late to save it.'

'Why did you insure your sister's life?'

'Because Mr Cooper pressed me to do so. I said I was very fond of my sister and wanted to give her a nice funeral if anything happened.'

'You say that you insured your sister's life so that you could give her a proper burial?'

'Yes.'

'Then why didn't you claim the body when you went to the asylum?'

Mary Ann (plausibly): 'I wanted to take her away to London to bury her amongst the rest of her friends in London, but when we went to Leavesden Asylum on March 16th they gave us such a peculiar interview with the doctors and nurses. First they said that she died suddenly, and then they said that she had been in the infirmary a week. Then how could she have died suddenly? Then they asked us about the cake, and we knew nothing about it. They seemed determined to keep the body, and seemed to think that death had occurred under peculiar circumstances, and pressed us to leave the body in their possession.'

Rawlinson arrived now at the matter of the invisible fiancé, which had been unwillingly introduced into the evidence by Mrs Molony at the police court. The desire to marry him seemed strongly to show motive; indeed it stood out as a recognisable human ambition from all the paler dross of rats and poison, handwriting and zymotic diseases. The Crown did not have to prove motive, as is quite well known, but motive is always relevant as evidence if it can be shown that the existence of a convincing motive makes it more likely that the defendant did actually commit the crime. For some reason, Clarke Hall had not brought Mr X into his client's life-or-death evidence in some reducing or sanitizing way. He must have known that the prosecution would be bound to explore this promising area, and she was exposed on a rock to cope with the moment. At least, surely, he must have warned her to be prepared?

Counsel: 'Now you say you did not want any clothing or money. Were you engaged to be married?'

'I was.'

'Was that standing over until the two of you had enough to make up a home?'

'Well, there did not seem enough on the young man's side. The young man did not seem to have enough money to start housekeeping – not enough on the money he earned – and so it was postponed until such time as he got a better situation and earn more money.'

And there Mr Rawlinson let her go. Her own counsel chose not to re-examine, although he was entitled to do so. He announced that he proposed to call no more evidence. There were no character witnesses in waiting. It was known that there was inadequate funding for the defence. The logistics of finding suitable persons who had not already been called by the prosecution, going to them in inner London, or persuading them out to Hemel Hempstead, to take statements were presumably insuperable at that time. Mary Ann was of good character – had no previous convictions – and such witnesses, people in authority, perhaps clergy or teachers, could have contributed a valuable buffer. It was, no doubt, a surprise to the general public that the defence brought no witnesses in a capital trial run uncompromisingly on a Not Guilty plea.

However, Sir Edward Clarke called no evidence in the Adelaide Bartlett case of 1886, where there were ample funds, relying on his exhaustive and famous cross-examination of Dr Thomas Stevenson, that same expert who had just given evidence which weighed heavily now against Mary Ann Ansell. Marshall Hall was to call no evidence for George Joseph Smith (1915). He did comment that, 'Had the prisoner not been the pauper he is, had he been possessed of unlimited means, he might have procured experts to say that the cause of death was other than that stated by the expert for the Crown.'

Mary Ann was put back in the dock, and, all too soon, Mr Rawlinson was embarking on his closing speech. It was fair and measured. He said that the prosecution had to satisfy the jury on two points – that the cause of death was poisoning, especially by phosphorus, and that it was the prisoner who had administered it. He thought that the jury could not have the slightest doubt that the death was from phosphorus. The evidence of the doctors was clear, especially that of Dr Stevenson, the eminent specialist, who, in answer to the suggestion of learned counsel for the defence, that the deceased had died from yellow atrophy, had said that disease was very rare and that in this case the symptoms and effects were rather of phosphorus. He had testified that the viscera showed signs of phosphorus poisoning. The very meaning of the word 'atrophy' was a shrinking of the liver, and that was not present here.

If the jury were once satisfied that the death was from poison by phosphorus, they could have no doubt that it was administered by the person – whoever that person was – who wrote the letter signed 'Harriett Parish'. No one else could have had any motive. The person who wrote that letter wrote the address on the brown paper parcel. On that point they had expert evidence, and the writing had been before them. Photographs of the documents had been submitted to the jury. They could judge for themselves. As to the insurance policy on her sister's life, although the prisoner was not in want of money for necessities and clothing, there was the fact that she wanted to get married. If she wanted to poison her sister, had she the means of doing it? Well, they had clear evidence on that point, for in January, February, and early March, she was undoubtedly in possession of phosphorus.

If the deceased was poisoned, who had the slightest interest in her life? The prisoner had insured her life, and she would be unlike the rest of civilised mankind if she were absolutely without the desire for money. It was for the jury to say what they had thought of her explanation for the purchase of phosphorus, but it would seem strange that a woman like Mrs Molony, who was always about the house, never had an inkling either of the getting of the rat poison or of its use. In conclusion, Counsel submitted that there was a motive for poisoning, that there was opportunity, and that there was a means of carrying it out. If they were satisfied with the evidence of the phosphorus, the jury would find that the cause of death was phosphorus poisoning, that it was administered in the cake, and that the cake was sent by the prisoner.

Then it was up to William Clarke Hall to save Mary Ann, and the press reported that he made an impassioned speech, but he was no successful Sir Charles Russell, defending Mrs Florence Maybrick, his 'friendless lady in the dock' in 1889, who called exhaustive medical evidence in a well-funded case, which, in spite of a verdict of Guilty of poisoning her husband with arsenic, raised such an intricate edifice of doubt that it was sufficient to secure a reprieve. Clarke Hall had it all to do himself, and the defence would have been greatly strengthened by expensive expert evidence on yellow atrophy, first floated by Percy Wisbey, and the absence of phosphorus in the body. There was no rhetorical appeal to the jury: his client was not an attractive figure. The case was still circumstantial, he said and the connecting links were missing. The whole case of proof rested upon the handwriting and he thought that the jury would be reluctant to jump to conclusions about, for example, the Harriett Parish letter. The conduct of the accused throughout had not been that of a guilty person. If she were guilty, would she not have kept the fact of having insured her sister's life locked up in the secret chamber of her own heart? Certainly! She would not have told her mistress about it the same day. Counsel used old-fashioned language to make this point, but the fact was that the insurance agent was a frequent visitor to the house in Great Coram Street, and the Molonys would have found out in the natural course of things. A really cunning girl would have gone to another company. Clarke Hall continued: the accused went to the asylum to see the body of her sister. If she had been guilty, would she have gone boldly to see her handiwork lying stiff and cold? If she had been guilty, would she have been so cool in the presence of such an appalling tragedy? Her evidence in court had not been shaken in cross-examination. It was normal for persons in her state of life to have a morbid horror of a relative's being buried by the parish.

Returning to a favourite medical topic, Counsel said that yellow atrophy was a known disease, and, a triumphant new fact, that it was more likely to attack unmarried women. (Although he had been trounced on yellow atrophy, he was taking a chance that the jury might not have fully understood, and, anyway, that there was still mileage in it.) It certainly did appear doubtful, he now said hopefully, whether it was possible to distinguish the symptoms of acute yellow atrophy from those of phosphorus poisoning. (The obstacle here was still that it was beyond the bounds of possibility that all the inmates had been stricken with the same disease, suddenly, at the same time.

Nor was it contagious.) His suggestion, he now said, was that the deceased (alone) was suffering from the preliminary stages of acute yellow atrophy and that she and the other women had partaken of some kind of poison - some mysterious disease which had not yet been discovered. There had been a 'strange outbreak' of enteritis and the doctors were agreed in thinking that enteritis was caused by some kind of poisoning.

The jury must have thought that this dialectical brainwave was far-fetched. Clarke Hall was cautious when he turned to the motive: he 'thought he was right' in saying that if there had been no motive shown the jury would never have been troubled with the case. The topic of 'motive', already mentioned in these pages, was always open to discussion. Sir James Fitzjames Stephen, summing up in the Maybrick case, put the matter usefully: 'I do not myself think that it is always possible to assign a motive, or that it is always desirable to do so. If you cannot find a motive, well you can't, and you must consider the fact without the light that motive would throw upon it. But when clear evidence of motive can be given, that clear evidence is a matter of the very first importance to consider.'

Therefore, said Clarke Hall, always adverting to the circumstantial chain, the whole weight of the case (and he was not challenged on this) hung on the motive, and the insurance for £11 was an inconceivably inadequate motive. It was true, he said, that he was unable to point to any other person who had any such motive – he knew of none, he suggested none – but, at the same time when the prosecution asked them to take the motive which they put forward, it was for them to look into all the bearings of that motive. The prisoner had been perfectly frank in saying that her marriage was put off because her fiancé was not in a position to marry. The postponement was only suggested in February, 1899, whereas the insurance was affected in September, 1898. (The date of the postponement was not actually in evidence.) The sum of £11 would go a very little way in the getting of a home together to live comfortably, even for people in a humble station of life. (Counsel was on shifting sands here. The patrician classes failed to understand that, for the 'humbler classes', a lump sum amounting to nearly a year's wages, when saving was an impossibility, whichever century or decade we are in, was a substantial gain. Someone with a background in charitable work should have known that.)

It had been proved, Counsel moved on, that each bottle of the phosphorus paste contained enough poison to kill three adults, so what possible motive could the prisoner have had (if guilty) for purchasing five separate bottles? Surely it was natural for a servant who slept in the kitchen, where her mistress admitted that there were rats, to seek to destroy them? (By wholesale methods, he could have added.) Moreover, if she had evil intent, would she have gone to a shop near to where she lived, and where she was perfectly well known? As for the tea and sugar, could the jury believe that they contained phosphorus, if they indeed had poison at all in them? Dr Stevenson had testified that he could not suggest any way in which the paste could have been put in without the taste being noticeable. (Rawlinson had studiously not included the tea parcel in his closing address, as being not evidentially satisfactory.)

As for the cake, it was true that the prisoner had the opportunity of making it, but was it really poisoned? 'Great stress was laid on the yellowness of the cake, but, as a matter of fact, *the phosphorus paste was even more white in colour than ordinary flour.*' This was a most bizarre, new assertion, and, anyway, out of place in a closing speech. The cake that reached the ward clearly *was* yellow, from the evidence of the prosecution witnesses who had seen it. There had been no defence witnesses. 'Taylor', the Bible of first reference, first published in 1865, was revised by Dr Thomas Stevenson himself in 1883. Here it is stated that 'the rat-pastes contain 2 per cent yellow phosphorus, sugar and bran.'

Why would Clarke Hall have spoken of 'the' phosphorus paste? How could he know what was in the cake? The explanation may be that he had been reading up on phosphorus, and had seen that yellow phosphorus begins in its pure state as solid white phosphorus. However, once cut into, adulterated, mixed, it turns into yellow phosphorus. His research had not been deep enough. If he had been more persevering, he would, too, have seen the possibilities of the absence of the classical signs of phosphorus poisoning, namely luminosity and a 'garlicky' smell. Dr Stevenson would have been expecting Clarke Hall to cross-examine him rigorously on this point, but no such words came forth.

(The colourant, Prussian blue, added as a warning of poison content, was, we know, present in the rat poison sold by Mr Noakes in Marchmont Street. By what witchery, then, did Mary Ann Ansell letch out the dark, vivid blue colour to make a semblance of a cream sponge? Was that feasible? Would she have bought so many bottles in order to *experiment*? Was she clever enough? Or could she have bought another brand elsewhere that did not contain Prussian blue?)

Finally, the flow of Clarke Hall's wisdom dried up. Percy Wisbey sat behind his barrister with a feeling of doom, but there was always hope. The judge summed-up for three-quarters of an hour. (Mr Justice Stephen, in *Maybrick*, took two days.) The summing-up was against Mary Ann Ansell. He said that learned counsel for the defence had struggled manfully to upset the evidence by the yellow atrophy suggestion, but in this case the liver was of normal size. It was an astonishing thing that four people at the asylum should be seized with a disease of the rarest kind at the same moment. On the point of the handwriting, the jury must not look too much for resemblance of single letters, but judge its appearance on the whole. If the jury looked at the writing on the Christmas card, the cake wrapper, the letter to the insurance agent, and the questions which the prisoner had written for the inquest, they ought to come to the conclusion that they were all written by the same person; but they must judge about that for themselves. Dr Stevenson, who was one of the greatest analysts of the day, had said that it was decidedly a case of phosphorus poisoning. The prisoner had made mis-statements and misrepresentations on taking out the insurance policy. If she were guilty of this offence – one of the greatest enormity – the jury could have no sympathy with her, because for the sake of a few pounds she had been willing to sacrifice the life of her poor sister.

The jury must exercise their ordinary powers of reason, and be guided by their consciences whatever the consequences might be.

The jury were sent out just before the luncheon adjournment, and deliberated for sixty-five minutes. They were anxious, tired after a bad night, homesick, and hungry, but they were conscientious, and they were going to be put under pressure by an impatient judge: that was not supposed to happen. When they returned, unable to agree upon their verdict, Mr Justice Mathew told them, 'Then I want to hear nothing from you. You must retire again. This is not a case in which you can be discharged because, after a short discussion, you have not been able to agree. Can I assist you by reading over any of the depositions?' The foreman began to explain something, presumably to give reasons for the disagreement, but the judge interrupted him, saying that he would not hear it. The foreman said that the jury did not want to hear depositions.

Another juror asked if they might have some refreshments, but the judge denied their request. Starvation of the jury was not an inhumanity peculiar to Judge Mathew. There was a long history of the practice. A letter to the *Watford Observer* (January 7th, 1899) from Mr WDL Beaumont suggested

> an alteration of the law which deprives a jury in such cases of refreshments till they have arrived at their verdict. They are now often compelled to hurry their verdict from a feeling of exhaustion, when "rational refreshments" would conduce to calmer deliberation and possibly to a different conclusion.

Similarly, the writer of an anonymous letter to the *Pall Mall Gazette* (July 6th, 1899), quoting Pope's line, 'And wretches hang that jurymen may dine' said of the Ansell jury that, 'Their deliberations would have probably lasted longer if their supplies had not run short. Plainly, they had some difficulty in arriving at a decision, and the judge "rushed" them.'

'A solicitor' addressing the Editor of the *Daily Mail* (July 12th, 1899) complained that,

> Jurymen at assizes suffer abominably. It frequently happens, that a judge will sit on until ten or twelve o'clock at night before he

discharges the jurymen, and then what happens? The jury are many miles from their homes, there are no trains or conveyances to be had at that time of the night. They have either to walk or put up in the town at their own expense. To talk of justice being done at ten o'clock at night, with everyone tired, hungry and cross, to put it mildly, is wicked.

As the Hertford jury left their box, undoubtedly disgruntled, there was a 'great commotion' in court. They were out for another hour. The defence felt a stirring of hope. The judge told the court that the jury were sending to him for documents one by one. He thought that they had been furnished with all the documents. Now he considered that the best thing to do would be to have them back in court and to read over to them all the documents from beginning to end. A palpable threat. The Clerk of Arraigns took one final document to the jury in their room, and they capitulated and returned a few minutes later, at 3.28, with a verdict of GUILTY.

His Lordship assumed the black cap. He looked at Mary Ann, who remained impassive. He spoke:

> It is impossible that the jury, as reasonable and conscientious men, should return any other verdict than the verdict of guilty. It has been shown to their satisfaction that you deliberately took the life of your sister, an afflicted woman, who had never been a burden to you, and who had the utmost claim upon your affection and compassion. Never in my experience has so terrible a crime been committed for a motive so utterly inadequate. It is no part of my duty to add to the misery of your position by words of opprobrium, but I feel bound to warn you that you must be prepared to follow your victim. Time will be allowed you, and I hope it will be employed in seeking mercy where alone mercy can surely be found.

He passed sentence of death in the usual form, and the chaplain said Amen. The court which had been hushed and solemn was suddenly filled with the screams of the mother, waiting outside, who had been told the news, followed by the reciprocal wailing of the condemned girl. The court reporters failed to agree on her exact words in the commotion, from 'That's my mother!' to 'Murder!' The docile legal puppet had become a living person, soon to die, who was calling for her mother. The piercing noise, and the pity and terror, affected many who were present, not only the women. Afterwards, the general public objected to the judge's warning that Mary Ann could not expect temporal mercy,[15] but the words were in fact a form of legal code, a stamp, to indicate that the judge intended to advise against any commutation of death sentence. Anyway, she was not mentally equipped to have understood the significance of 'alone', any more than 'opprobrium' would have meant anything at all to her. In reality, the judge was addressing the official and legal world at large, not the girl in the dock.

A reminiscent journalistic account has an authentic feeling:

> In the dock to my left stood a woman of twenty-two. Her dark hair was untidy: her face was lean. She had tense, black eyes .... I saw the chaplain place the black cap on the head of Mr Justice Mathew, who sat to my right, underneath those three square-topped windows .... As the judge spoke the words of the death sentence the quavering notes of a street organ of those days came through the open windows.[16]

The court was quickly cleared, and the crowd of spectators dispersed gradually from the precinct, shaken, and wanting to talk about what they had just experienced. Many stayed to see Mary Ann being taken back to St Albans gaol. Inside, the court was re-set, and the judge still sat as a commonplace civil case was called on – a claim for detention of goods near Potters Bar.

The fact is, that there had been rumours of something wrong, and, behind the scenes, the ruffled defence lawyers were in urgent conference. Eventually, that evening, Percy Wisbey emerged and told the waiting press that a petition would be sent to the Home Secretary, praying that the death sentence might be commuted on the grounds of insanity.

---

15 Compare with: 'the Lord Chief Baron, in passing sentence, omitted to tell the prisoner that there was no hope, and he should prepare to leave this world. This was always done in cases where the judge intended to advise against any commutation of the sentence.' Leonard A Parry (ed.), *Trial of Dr Smethurst*, (William Hodge, 1931), p. 16.
16 *Daily Express*, 20 July 20 1938.

CHAPTER SIX

THE WEDDING GOWN

There had been a fundamental, a mortal misjudgement in the conduct of the defence. The fatal impediment to a late submission of insanity was that it was supposed to be put at the earliest opportunity, at the head of the hearing, where you could argue it to your heart's content and bring a string of witnesses. The plea of insanity was not to be offered as a neck-saving after-thought, which was not particularly likely to succeed. Here, the defence had burnt their boats, and, worse, the judge had already stamped Mary Ann as unfit for mercy. He saw her as an ordinary, low-class Assize malefactor, differing only in her degree of exceptional wickedness. According to the *Dictionary of National Biography*, however, it was said that he showed a slight leaning towards the accused.

To the general public, Mary Ann, only a servant, seemed to be represented by a full, effective defence team. Clarke Hall had two juniors with him. One was Mr Theobald Mathew, who appears to have been the judge's elder son. The *DNB* has full profiles of father and son. No other barrister of that name, practising at that time, has been traced. This close relationship appears curious in a capital case, but no doubt the presumption of the judge's impartiality prevails. Clarke Hall himself, however impassioned and medically well prepared, was not experienced in such a grave case. Only *The Times* reported that a third barrister was in court for the defence, Mr R Swaby: to take a note, no doubt.

The instructing solicitor, ridiculously young, used to minor 'High Street' offences, out of his depth, with no apparent clerk to help him, and minimum funding, was growing up rapidly under a monstrous burden. The barrister had accepted the brief at its face-value. It was unusual at that time for counsel to hold pre-trial conferences with clients in capital cases, so that Clarke Hall had probably not assessed Mary Ann face-to-face, before the trial, but in-depth discussion between the two lawyers did occur.[17] It would have been in character for Clarke Hall to have been overbearing with the provincial, novice solicitor.

Away from the black and white certainties of the court, there had been a growing movement, a suspicion, that Mary Ann's mental state was not normal, fuelled by the vital information elicited from the Molonys, weeks previously, by the *Daily Mail*, scenting a story and an issue. The defence had not picked up those strong words that Mary Ann was of *very limited intelligence*. Insanity, as we have said, often covered both the mentally ill and the mentally handicapped. There were a number of responsible people in the community who had much to impart about the girl, but had never been asked. To them, and they were now extremely worried, the trial had revealed only a portion of the whole picture.

Mary Ann Ansell did not look quite right. Everyone could see that. Her facial features were recognisably those of someone born with a degree of defect. Her much commented upon, removed demeanour in court, most of the time, caused concern. Some thought that the actual nature of the crime, the perceived inadequacy of the motive, her indifference to the consequences of the use of deadly poison, the silliness, and yet cunning, of the plan, showed insanity to the ultimate degree, but others could not get past the premeditation, the second attempt at the crime, the disguised handwriting, even if poorly executed, and the thought-out device of the 'Harriett Parish' letter. Then she lied stoutly in the witness box, with all the sang-froid of a practised criminal. She knew exactly when to deny things put to her.

There was as yet no Court of Criminal Appeal (to be set up in

17 For this information see Andrew Rose, *The Prince, the Princess and the Perfect Murder* (2013), p. 275.

1907) although it was at that time much canvassed. There was already a strong body of opinion that favoured the abolition of capital punishment. The hanging of women was widely regarded as repugnant, long before the final one, the execution of Ruth Ellis in 1955. The only available route of appeal in 1899 was a petition to the Home Secretary for a commutation of sentence. The decision rested ultimately on the conscience of one man. Theoretically, as last resort, the Queen could be petitioned, beseeching her to exercise her Royal Prerogative, but, however heartrending the pleas to Her Majesty, in practice, she would always refer the matter back to her Home Secretary. Her people did not know that.

Sir Matthew White Ridley was her man at this particular time. How was he going to deal with his unpleasant duty? A wealthy landowner, a Conservative to the core, a perfect model of the ruling classes, he was moderately, not passionately, philanthropic. Born in 1842, fifth baronet of Blagdon, Northumberland, Harrow and Balliol, nine years a fellow of All Souls, called to the Inner Temple in 1864, he was an intellectual by inclination. His mother died of tuberculosis in 1845, and his childhood at Blagdon was 'lonely and severe.' (*DNB*) He was Salisbury's Home Secretary from 1895 to 1900, and made no great mark. 'His political career failed to fulfil the promise of his youthful academic brilliance.' (*DNB*) He was the Home Secretary who agreed to Oscar Wilde's request for books in Reading gaol, but refused early release.

1899 was Ridley's *annus horribilis*. His wife, born in 1850, died unexpectedly on March 14th, the cause of death blood-poisoning, after a severe attack of influenza. Ridley sat for two days at her bedside in their opulent town house, 10 Carlton House Terrace. The eldest son was summoned back from his honeymoon in Egypt. Her death was known to be a terrible blow to Ridley. She, the Honourable Mary Georgiana was said to be the incarnation of kindness, of truly philanthropic nature. Only three months later, in Mary Ansell he saw a young woman who had wilfully killed her own sister. It is absolutely fair to speculate that if his wife had lived, a disposition to mercy might have tempered his resolve to uphold the decision of the Court.

In 1895, when he had inherited the handling of the vexatious Florence Maybrick cause – to obtain her release – from his predecessor, Asquith, he had disappointed many by not being dynamic in initiating a fresh enquiry. In 1899, there appeared a work, entitled *The Necessity for Criminal Appeal: As illustrated by the Maybrick Case and the Jurisprudence of Various Countries*, edited by JH Levy (PS King and Son), in which Sir Matthew White Ridley was strongly criticised. Having said in the House that he would promise to take up the case to the best of his ability, he kept Mrs Maybrick incarcerated during his term. Levy said that no one could pretend that Ridley made a serious attempt to elucidate the problems, and that the 'implied proofs of guilt' had been kept back, with Mrs Maybrick locked away on the strength of a secret dossier.

In the Ansell case, the culture of secrecy prevailed, and The Home Office file reveals hidden opinions which would have shocked the general public. The burden of the work done and decisions made is seen to be undertaken largely by Sir Kenelm Digby, Ridley's permanent Under-secretary of state, a civil servant, although matters judged to be of the greatest importance were minuted 'seen by Secretary of State' (i.e. the Home Secretary). Sir Kenelm Edward Digby (1836–1916), Harrow, Corpus Christi, Oxford, called to the bar 1865, son of a clergyman, was primarily a lawyer, and a liberal, to boot, believing in 'the greater importance of giving substantial power to the working classes.' Ridley and Digby were not, therefore, constitutionally like-minded.

The execution chariot hurried on: the Under-sheriff for Hertfordshire wrote to the Home Office on July 1st, so soon, requiring copies of the appropriate regulations for a judicial hanging, and asking for the name of the most reliable executioner. The judge's not very full, plain notes of the trial evidence were copied up by a clerk and despatched to the Home Office. On July 4th, the Home Office sent a telegram to the Governor of St Albans gaol, requesting a copy newspaper report of the trial, and thus began its own collection of trial and post-trial press material. In contemplation of trouble ahead, depositions from both coroner's and magistrates' courts were got in.

The *Daily Mail* was preparing for an intensive campaign. In a resounding leader of July 3rd, Mary Ann's self-possession was viewed as the calmness of *moral paralysis*, a current term, which was descriptive enough. The sheer inadequacy of the motive raised suspicion of her 'mental equilibrium'. The appeal was to the conscience of the nation, protesting on the grounds of her sex and her youth. It could not be pretended that at twenty-two, this half-educated and forlorn creature was a hardened, hopeless criminal. Let justice be tempered with mercy.

The Metropolitan Asylums Board never succeeded in arriving at a united front in the matter, determined to remain out of the debate and protect the interests of the Board. They had, even so, to contend with a persistent activist, in the person of the Reverend GW Pope, who declared at a meeting of the body on the last day of the Ansell trial that 'Anyone who knew anything about the case must be aware that the woman was not in a proper mental condition.' He asked if it was intended to communicate with the Home Secretary. The Chairman, Sir Edward Galsworthy, (1831–1920) said, 'This is altogether irregular. You can give notice of motion.'

Mr Pope: 'To consider the matter this day fortnight?'

Chairman: 'Yes.'

Mr Pope: 'But the girl might be hanged in that time, or at least beyond the chance of receiving the benefits which our efforts might secure her.' In the end, the MAB remained neutral. Galsworthy resigned from the board in 1901.

The *Western Times* contributed some considered points: the jury had been seeking some loophole to save the girl, and

> Young girls, as medical law testifies, are occasionally under influences which render them irresponsible for their acts. In the present case it is certain that there is a taint of lunacy in the family, and it may be lurking in the prisoner. On no other ground is it possible to adequately account for her extraordinary behaviour. She did not act in a manner that would suggest that she wished to hide anything. Everything was open and above board. She purchased the

poison at the shop where she was perfectly well known... In some quarters a modification of the law so as to give judges more latitude in its application to varying degrees of murder is demanded.

On that same day, there appeared in the *Daily Mail* the first part of the dossier which that paper was compiling as to Mary Ann's mental state. This was pioneering stuff, a marker in the race against time, and the Home Office looked on with increasing concern. A reporter had gone to Tankerton Street, whither no lawyer had ventured, on Monday July 3rd, and accosted some neighbours, not named, who were happy to be interviewed. They knew Mary Ann very well, they said, and on many occasions 'she clearly showed symptoms of a very weak mind.' 'I can assure you,' one person informed the man from the *Daily Mail*, 'that insanity runs in the family. Take Mary Ann. I've always said that she was not quite right.' The reporter was making careful notes:

> She never seemed to know what she was doing. She would go to children playing in the street and shake them for no cause whatever. She would also speak to you in a silly manner. Once she followed my husband into the yard and shouted "Bah! Bah!" She continued to follow and shout until I said, "Get away," and then she stared at me in a vacant kind of way, as if she didn't understand a bit what she had been doing or saying. I'm told there was a good deal of insanity on the mother's side, and as I've said, you can easily see that some of the children are not quite right.

This is not the Mary Ann whom the judge saw, nor, presumably, her lawyers. The only area of doubt might be that the neighbour was remembering the wrong Ansell girl.

In addition to the 'official', legal petition, a determined supporter, Mr W Jobson, making his first appearance in the matter, announced that he, too, intended to formulate a separate petition on the grounds of insanity. He is one of the possible contributors to the defence fund. Living at 2, Charlton Street, NW, off the Euston Road, near the Somerstown Ansells, including Harriett Parish and her family, he was said to have an intimate acquaintance with the Ansells.

On that first Monday, after a weekend of torment, James and Sarah took a train to St Albans to see their condemned daughter, not getting home until late at night. The next day, the reporter was back to find out how they had got on.

> "We have had a hard time," said Mr Ansell dully. "First we had to put away one daughter – that's the one that's dead, and then we have another child who's mad", and he pointed to a girl aged about sixteen years old [Martha]. "Now we are waiting to know whether another is to be hung as a murderess, or pronounced insane. I can't give any opinion. I am in a maze. I can't conceive that one sister killed the other. They were both good girls. We never had any trouble with them, and they seemed very fond of each other. I really cannot say whether I think Mary Ann insane or not. If anything could be done to prove her not right in the head, I should only be too thankful. Anything rather than her present fate. But I cannot and will not express any opinion. It's not for me to judge betwixt the living and the dead."

After these dignified words, Sarah Ansell amplified the painful truths, the family secrets:

> "My husband's mother had fits from the time she was five years old, and she lived to a great age. They were caused by her being put into a dark cellar. On my side, of course, there were my two aunts, my mother's sisters. They both died quite mad in asylums. Then there's my daughter, who's dead, and there's Martha, another daughter, who's mad, too. As for Mary Ann, she was a good girl, though she was always queer. Sometimes she'd speak to me and sometimes she wouldn't. Once she wouldn't speak to me for two years. Sometimes with all the trouble I feel as if I should go mad myself. As for what I thought of her yesterday: I was so upset that I hardly knew what was happening." And Mrs Ansell began to sob anew.

So, the *Daily Mail* concluded, 'In the poor little home in Tankerton Street, the stricken parents cling to the fact that Mary was "always queer" in the hope of a reprieve. Mary Ann completely broke down when she saw her parents through the grille of her cell door, with further access denied. She made no confession to them, and the crime was not much referred to, in case she became more upset. "I am prepared to meet my Maker," she said, "but I hope a petition will be got up for me." It was thought that she seemed to realise her awful position more keenly than she had since her arrest. She wept copiously when her parents had to leave her in her misery.'

Percy Wisbey had also seen the convicted girl in her cell. Horrified by the outcome, he was totally intent on trying to save her, probably turning away such other work as came to him and quite therefore out-of-pocket.

The *Daily Mail* was beginning to publish letters from the public which grew into a sizeable portfolio, many carried away in fulsome prose. For balance, there was a judicious admixture of adverse opinion. A 'spectator during the whole of the trial' wrote that, 'The conduct of the prisoner showed no signs whatever of "moral paralysis." She gave evidence on her own behalf with complete coolness and even occasional volubility. Was it likely that if there had been mental weakness, her extremely able counsel would not have made the most of it?' Some suggested diagnoses, such as 'advanced Hysteria'.

A concurrent stream of letters from individuals and various associations was now coming into the Home Secretary's office, all suing for mercy. If the pleas came from the professional classes, they were politely acknowledged, but 'irresponsible' contributions came to be destroyed. The Howard Association, instigated for the promotion of the best methods of Penal Treatment and Crime Prevention, merely, at this stage, forwarded loaded extracts from the *Daily Mail*. Pressure was fast building on the Home Office, and they fell back on the holy grail of precedence, compiling pages of annotated lists for the assistance of Sir Matthew: female murderers convicted of murder by poisoning since 1846, including Alice Hewitt (aged 27) who poisoned her mother with arsenic (1863) in order to realise a policy of life insurance; Mary Ann Cotton (aged 34) executed for life insurance murders, in particular of her stepson, aged eight, noted 'several petitions received'; Mary Britland (aged 39) who poisoned Mary Dixon to marry Dixon (1886) and get insurance money, with comment by (Sir) Godfrey Lushington, the Permanent Under Secretary at that time: 'The murder was committed by a woman and women are rarely executed, but the case is so grave (she murdered her husband and daughter and her neighbour's wife, by poison) that there ought to be no remission,' executed; Elizabeth Berry (aged 31) 1887, 'infirmary nurse poisoned her child with sulphuric acid to get insurance money. Coroner's jury also found she had poisoned her mother with atrophine a year before – Body exhumed', executed. Further, a list of all executions in 1896 and 1897 was provided, with quantitative annotations regarding the nature and size of petitions: e.g. 'Two big petitions, a few letters'; 'several petitions (large and small'; 'a few letters, no big petitions'; 'several petitions and letters.' 'He petitioned himself' and so on.

On July 5th, the Home Office received from the Director of Public Prosecutions, as requested, copies of the depositions, together with newspaper reports of the trial. A three-page summary of the proceedings was made, and approved by Kenelm Digby. The short point was that, 'The evidence is circumstantial but leaves no apparent doubt of the prisoner's guilt.' The principal points of the Crown case were set out, and then the main issue in hand:

> It is said in the newspapers that the question of insanity in the family is to be raised. There was nothing said about it at the trial. It may be well in anticipation of interview with learned judge on Monday or Tuesday to obtain a medical report from the Surgeon of the Prison. Also ask Police to get authentic information as to age. That is, the best they can. NB: The parents live in London.

It had been wrongly bruited that Mary Ann was only 18, and the Home Office, believing her to be 22, as she herself had testified, was anxious to scotch this line of mitigation once and for all. Laborious correspondence with the CID, New Scotland Yard, led to a visit by PS Alfred Ball to Tankerton Street, where the parents told him that Mary Ann had been born on November 8th, at 4 Dutton Street (Tankerton Street) and was 22 years old. PS Ball went next to the local registrar's office at 10 Argyle Square, to verify the date, but because of the lapse of time, was referred to Somerset House. The registrar's daughter said that she had known the Ansell family for a long time, and she believed that 22 years was correct. A certificate would cost 3s 7d. The Home Office perused all this, and Charles Stewart Murdoch made a note that, 'It seems pretty clear that the woman is 22, and hardly necessary to get the actual certificate.' He was overruled, however, by Sir Kenelm Digby, who did require the certificate to be acquired. It was going to be some time before this apparently simple matter was resolved.

The higher officials at the Home Office were mulling over their increasing file of lists, abstracts, letters and minutes, fortifying the traditional stance of very rarely departing from capital sentence. When they wrote to St Albans prison to enquire about Mary Ann Ansell's health, a reply, dated July 7th came from Edward Lloyd, Chief Warder: the prisoner's mental and physical condition were good, and at no time had she shown any symptoms of being of weak mind. This was exactly the opinion that the Home Office had hoped for, but a complaint was minuted that, 'We should have heard from the Doctor himself – but as there is no actual allegation of insanity before HO as yet, perhaps this is sufficient for the present.' The Chief Warder defended himself – the Home Office letter was not clear and did not specify a report from the medical officer. Even so, this was a notable milestone because, as the first (if quasi) medical report since sentence, it set the tone.

By contrast, in the running, unofficial inquiry by the *Daily Mail*, on July 6th, a resounding coup, ignored (in writing) by the Home Office, appeared under the heading of *A Plea for Mercy*. A reporter had obtained new information from an unspecified source, probably the Molonys. A leader of the same issue, *Mary Ansell's Fate*, hints that Mr X has been seen and interviewed, but it is not properly substantiated:

> The young man who was 'keeping company' with the girl, but who, not unnaturally, shrinks from mention in this connection, gives an account of his hapless fiancée which wholly agrees with the testimony of the neighbours, and immensely strengthens the view that she is of exceedingly weak intellect.

The new information, the 'plea for mercy', was a bombshell, if true, and should, of course have been tested in court. Mary Ann, the piece related,

> had a strong and erroneous idea that her relatives were oppressing her, and on many occasions she expressed her anxiety to get rid of her imaginary trouble by setting up a home of her own. She bought various articles of furniture, and in the beginning of the year she told her friends that she was going to get married at Easter. Singularly

enough, and this fact goes far to prove her insanity – she did not mention a single word to the young man in question about this Easter marriage. One day [so the *Daily Mail* representative was informed], the young man saw her wearing what she said was HER WEDDING GOWN and when he expressed his surprise, she merely stared in a vacant way, and later on took off her wedding dress and replaced it with her everyday garment. She had even bought the new costume without the knowledge of her lover. Those who have intimate knowledge of the girl's strange acts are earnestly hoping that a reprieve will be granted.

There is something paranoid about this behaviour, nearing delusional, at the very least with a tendency to fantasising, which eroded the hard purity of the alleged 'motive'. On the other hand, many a girl has bought a white dress in anticipation, and even household goods, when the proposed husband has not been 'coming up to scratch'.

The *Pall Mall Gazette*, which did not scruple to report crime, was adopting an opposing attitude to the Ansell case and published on July 7th a succinct letter from 'Zeta', prominently filed by the Home Office:

> Dear Sir, Allow me, as a constant reader, heartily to endorse the remarks which you made against the reprieve of Mary Ansell. Here is a woman who commits a peculiarly atrocious murder, and she is to be reprieved because, say some, of the very atrocity of the crime; because, say these advocates in another place, two aunts and a sister were mad. A campaign has been commenced against the Home Secretary, presuming upon the real or supposed weakness of that Minister. If he yields to it, he will be encouraging deliberate, cold-blooded murder. Feeling there is none against the death penalty being carried out in this case. It is being manufactured, as anyone who knows anything of journalism can see.

On Friday, July 7th, it was announced that the Under-Sheriff for the County of Hertfordshire had fixed the date for the execution – Wednesday, July 19th.[18]

---

18 Tuesday, July 18th, had been the appointed date, but had had to be changed when it was realised that hangman Billington would not have time to get from Winchester to St Albans (and make all preparations) after despatching Charles Maidment on that day. See Nicholas Connell and Ruth Stratton, *Hertfordshire Murders* (2007), p. 95.

CHAPTER SEVEN

'SILLY OLD ANSELL'

Now, with the serious realisation that only twelve days remained, there was an urgency in all quarters. A reporter from the *Daily Chronicle* obtained an interview with Percy Wisbey, who told him about the petition, which was under preparation. He enumerated the grounds which would be subsumed in the argument: the family antecedents, his client's youth, the absence of sufficient motive, and her behaviour in court. She did not comprehend the gravity of her position until the last moment. From first to last, he said, there was no air of conscious guilt, simply a sullen indifference to all that was going on. Other incidents which had come to light after the trial tended to strengthen the case for insanity.

The spate of letters to the newspapers increased, and the Home Office read them, cut out neatly and pasted on to sheets of paper by minions. The insurance companies were castigated, as supporters cast around for excuses and explanations. The *Daily Mail* itself contributed a 'genealogical table' of the familial mental afflictions revealed by the Ansell parents. The newspaper had found out by some means that the medical officer at St Albans prison 'Cannot at present state anything definite as to the condition of the condemned girl's mind, and that it is practically certain that an examination as to her mental condition will be held at the instance of the Home Secretary at an early date.' The *Daily Mail* also provided a list of six recent reprieves.[19]

19 These were: Robert Coombes, aged 13, murdered his mother, 'insane'; George Davies, aged 16, murdered his father, 1890, while riding home in a pony chaise at Crewe with brother, Richard – executed. George reprieved – penal servitude for life; Catherine

Parliament was being drawn into the controversy. Mr Charles H Wilson tabled two questions for the Home Secretary: (1) whether he has given his sanction for the execution of Mary Ansell on July

Kempshall, London music hall singer, shot dead Edgar Swinton Holland, Liverpool merchant, while suffering from 'monomania' after a breach of promise action – sent to Broadmoor in 1877; John Watson Laurie, the Arran murderer, 1899, killed Edwin Robert Rose on Goatfell, 1889, no clear motive, insanity pleaded after trial – died in Perth Criminal Asylum, 1930; Richard Prince, famous case, stabbed William Terriss, leading actor, outside the Adelphi Theatre, 1877, while markedly paranoid. He was not, in fact, so much reprieved as found irresponsible by the jury after defence brought three medical experts: sent to Broadmoor.

The case most drawn upon to illustrate the unfairness of class distinction, in combination with a lesser degree of insanity than Mary Ann Ansell (very arguable) was the coetaneous crime committed by Miss Bertha Haggerton Peterson. The judge was again Mr Justice Mathew and this time the early presentation of insanity, with religious delusions, was well received by the Court. Miss Peterson, aged 45, the daughter of the late rector of the parish of Biddenden, Kent, bought a gun from the Army and Navy Stores and practised with it in her back garden. On February 5th, 1899, she lured to the Sunday School where she taught, John Whibley, a shoemaker, the object of her hatred. Inviting him to admire the picture 'The Good Shepherd', which she had bought as a second prong of her attack, she shot him in the back of the head as he obediently admired her gift to the school. It turned out that she had picked on a rumour strongly denied, that Whibley had assaulted a little girl at the Sunday School, and the matter filled her whole mind. She wrote to the Archbishop of Canterbury about it, and perused the Criminal Law Amendment Act. 'God commanded me to do this' she insisted, and refused to consider her murderous act a crime. Mr Dickens, QC, for the Crown, called Dr Davies, superintendent of the Kent County Asylum to attest to her attitude. She said that wicked men wanted to hang her, which was evidence of the extreme wickedness of men. Mr CF Gill, QC, (with Mr A Gill) put in the previous depositions of an aunt, unable to be present, where she had attested that the prisoner's mother had been eccentric, and an epileptic, while other near relatives were also mentally afflicted. The jury interrupted Mr Gill's address and delivered a verdict of Guilty, but with a rider that Miss Peterson was suffering from delusions. She was taken to Broadmoor, in excellent spirits, saying that she had been very happy in prison for 6 months. Nonetheless, she had told visiting friends that she would rather have been hanged than confined in any asylum for the rest of her life in a sentiment right after Mr Percy Wisbey's heart. See *Illustrated Police News*, 22 July 1899.

Additionally, on July 17th, the *Daily Mail* got up a strong list of reprieved women who had received clemency: Margaret Dixblancs, a servant, murdered her mistress, Madame Riel, in Park Lane in 1872 – penal servitude for life; Elizabeth Gibbons, shot her husband at Hayes, 1884 – penal servitude for life; Kate Marshall stabbed her sister in Spitalfields, 1898 – reprieved; Edith Marian Morell, aged 23, barmaid, killed James Rule at Newcastle, 1899 – penal servitude for manslaughter; Christiana Edmunds, the chocolate poisoner, obsessed with Dr Beard, carelessly killed a child, Sidney Albert Baker – sent to Broadmoor in 1872. The trial judge, Baron Martin, had commented that there was method in her madness. Mrs Edith Carew, high-born resident in Yokohama in 1896, cruelly poisoned her husband, not insane – reprieved and sent to prison until released in 1910.

19th, and (2) will he state how many women have been executed in the years 1896, 1897, 1898, and, in how many instances have memorials for mercy been refused. Sir Matthew White Ridley replied, 'As to the first paragraph, I must decline to answer any questions in the House as to the advice which it will be my duty to tender to Her Majesty. (Hear, hear) Thirty-five men and one woman [the noxious baby-farmer, Mrs Amelia Dyer]. In the great majority of these cases applications in some form for mercy were made.' Careful preparations for these loaded questions had been made by the civil servants, and finalised by Sir Kenelm Digby.

The *Daily Mail* (July 7th) featured expansive letters from the Molonys:

> I can truthfully say that neither my husband nor myself entertains any doubt as to Mary Ann Ansell's weak and irresponsible mind. During the time she was with me she seemed to grow decidedly worse. From being merely silly and at times vacant, as was shown by her mumbling to herself and her loud fits of laughter at nothing at all, she got to having hallucinations, and then became positively spiteful. Once she insisted on going out and engaging a room, to occupy when she was married, although her young man had not at that time so much as proposed marriage to her. She not only hired a room when there was no prospect of her being married, but went to work buying things to furnish it.
>
> The change in Mary Ann Ansell's mental state grew rapidly worse during the last year she was with me. She would go for days without speaking a word except when I addressed her concerning her duties, and she was cruel to her little sisters. One day her little brother came here to see her, and she beat him terribly, although he had done nothing to deserve it. One of her great amusements was to get a cat in the area [the front yard in the basement, behind the railings] and throw water on it. This would delight her so she shrieked with laughter. Faithfully yours, MS Molony.

The Molonys' loyalty to Mary Ann is remarkable; she was their maid-of-all work, not a relative. If they had been allowed to say what they knew at the court, the result could have been different, indeed. Is there exaggeration? Possibly. No one else had said or was going to say that there were hallucinations. They seem to have been trying to establish actual insanity, to back the petition, not some wishy-washy 'moral insanity', nor 'imbecility'. Much of the behaviour described in detail is, in fact, textbook 'mental deficiency', especially with the emotional lability, spitefulness and cruelty. Just to muddy the picture, symptoms of frank madness may sometimes be superimposed upon the basic deficiency: 'These psychoses whilst resembling the mature forms, are simple in nature. Depression, excitement, delusions and hallucinations may be noted. A number of high-grade defectives develop compensatory paranoid states. Schizophrenic disorders are not uncommon.' The authority here is Dr HC Beccle, who was the splendid Physician Superintendent of Springfield Psychiatric Hospital, Upper Tooting.[20]

Mr Molony had a number of observations of his own to add; in his eloquent, Irish style, his thoughts on the affair, which had previously been stifled, came out freely:

> I have always had an impression that she was more or less mentally deranged, though never could imagine her criminally inclined. I have noticed particularly her complete absence of the power of distinction between the condition of the station of one person and another. If we spoke of Her Majesty the Queen and paid her a high compliment for some good act, Mary would be able to readily discover the same kind of benevolence and condescension on the part of her own mother in some similar way; and any public man or society lady would always have this or that attribute similar to some member of Mary's family. She would say those things with such intense earnestness that left no doubt of her believing it herself. She would laugh immoderately, without the slightest reason, talk to herself when she fancied herself alone, having an imaginary row with some one or other [perhaps these were the "hallucinations"] weeping occasionally for something she imagined someone might do to herself or her friends.
>
> Altogether, I am quite convinced this unfortunate creature is mentally deficient and childish, and never seemed to me to have any notion of moral responsibility. She seemed to love her family with a passionate love and to hate them the same day with a most insensate hate. If Mary Ansell be not demented then she is the most complex character I have ever known or heard of. She seemed to have an enduring love for her mother, and scarcely ever railed about her. This was evidenced at the trial, when the cries of her mother seemed for the first time to awake her to a sense of her position, and it is scarcely

20   See *Psychiatry: Theory and Practice for Students and Nurses*, p. 252.

to be wondered at that she was infinitely touched for her mother, who has had a terribly unhappy time .... Truly this is a woman of sorrow, the hand of fate and the arm of the law destroying her poor offsprings before her eyes. Fate is inexorable, but human destruction can be stayed by the exercise of mercy and charity.

I hope the women of England, whose kindly and noble impulses have created a Florence Nightingale, a Grace Darling, and, of distant kindred, a Mrs Beecher Stowe, to make humanity more human and assuage the pain of the suffering, will rouse themselves to save this unhappy mother from the terror of adding to her long list of sorrow the degrading death of her child on the scaffold.

Emphasizing the childish deficiency of Mary Ann more than any grosser behaviour, Patrick Molony's use of Mary Ann's unusual attitude towards royalty may count as a benchmark of his sincerity and accuracy: no one would have invented this quirk in order to illustrate her abnormal thinking. A picture of her comportment and conversation was forming. She was not a normal member of society, nor a happy one. The *Daily Mail* mused that, 'Possibly the very strength of the case for the girl's insanity may have created a false sense of security.' This newspaper's representative was sent out to find Mary Ann's former teachers. At 112 Westbourne Terrace, he ran to earth Miss Frost, who, he said carefully, was a woman of great guardedness of speech.

Eight years ago I was teacher of a Sunday School class which included Mary Ansell. The class was held in the parish of St Pancras, and for two or three years she was a pupil. At that period I must say that no doubt of Mary Ansell's sanity entered my mind; but looking back now I can recall an irresponsibility and vacancy of her demeanour which may have been evidence of mental disturbance. In no way could she be termed a girl of high intelligence, and she impressed me as being good-hearted, and at times preternaturally acute and cunning.

The *Daily Mail* also, (July 9th) located Mrs GW Ayres, at her home in Tufnell Park. She was employed at the Brecknock Board School, York Road, Camden, but she had previously taught Mary Ann at the Manchester Street Board School in 1886-7. She would have had a better opportunity than a Sunday School teacher to observe her pupil. She said:

> I had Mary Ann Ansell in my class for a considerable time. I always
> looked upon her as one of feeble, if not irresponsible, mind. It is a
> little difficult to pick out at this distance of time any set of things
> from which one could positively state that the girl was insane, but
> there were a number of little oddities, which, considered together,
> would leave almost anyone with no doubt as to the state of this poor
> girl's mental powers. Perhaps one of the most noticeable of Mary Ann
> Ansell's peculiarities was the fact that I could never place her behind
> any of the other children, because of her unconquerable desire to
> stick pins into them. Of course I have known of other children being
> addicted to this practice, but only as a mischievous trick. With Mary
> it was a besetting habit.
>
> Another peculiarity was that when she was scolded for anything,
> she did not sulk in the ordinary sense of the word, but when offended
> in any way by a casual remark, her papers and work generally,
> instead of being properly done, would resemble the marks made
> by a fly on piece of paper after it had been soaked in the ink-bottle.
> At other times she could do her writing well enough. When Mary
> had one of her bad fits she was extraordinary in her demeanour
> when addressed. She would on no account answer, no matter what
> pressure was put on her. All she would do would be to glare at you,
> as if she did not know what you were talking about. She had a most
> insane look at these times, and would stare out from under her half-
> closed lids in the strangest way.

As a matter of fact, this could have been the petit mal of epilepsy,
which a teacher could not have been expected to recognise. This is
the only account of such appearances in Mary Ann, but poisoned
Caroline was a known epileptic.

> Of course [Mrs Ayres continued], these may seem little things, but,
> putting them all together, one could only arrive at the conclusion that
> the girl was out of her mind – at least, at times. I was so impressed
> with the girl's general irresponsibility that I never punished her for
> her misbehaviour or faults as I should have other girls. I can frankly
> say that I did not consider her responsible for what she did. Mary
> Ann Ansell was the kind of child who would now be educated at
> what are called the Special Schools. Children of her sort frequently
> do all sorts of queer things, and I have no doubt that if Mary killed
> her sister she did it when she was in one of her moods, and does
> not properly realize that she did it. I have been fourteen years a
> certificated teacher, and have had in that time 1,200 children put

through my hands. I have never had a normal child act as Mary Ann Ansell did when she was under my care.

This vitally important report was filed without comment at the Home Office, but then that Office held the view that this sort of thing was only hearsay.

The chaplain at St Albans gaol, the Reverend Henry Fowler, who was seen as 'aged', was induced to grant an interview with the *Daily Mail*, which he afterwards regretted. 'I really cannot say,' he told the reporter, 'that the unfortunate girl comprehends the guilt of the crime of which she has been convicted. I have visited her daily, and have talked and read to her in the ministration of religious comfort, but it is very difficult to say, and I really cannot say that she understands the gravity of her offence.' These were the words, coming from a man of the cloth, used to dealing with convicts, which greatly troubled the public mind and fermented the 'agitation'.

> She seems to be quite glad for me to talk to her, [the cleric went on miserably] and she certainly grasps the fact that she may be hanged, but she does not seem at all to comprehend the serious nature of the crime. It is certainly one of the most difficult cases I have ever had to deal with. She does not acknowledge that she caused her sister's death - in fact, it is almost impossible to get her to say anything at all about her. It is only in a half-comprehending way that she refers to the matter, and it is really extremely difficult to know whether she is in a condition to be held morally responsible for the crime. Of course, it is a medical question whether she is insane, but I have seen her and talked to her every day, and I cannot say that she comprehends the terrible nature of her position.

The reporter then took it upon himself to inform the clergyman about the history of insanity in the family. Mr Fowler was taken by surprise; he had known nothing about it, and obviously no one had thought that he ought to be aware of the background. He clearly did not read the *Daily Mail*, but he must have been unusually sheltered from the talk of the staff at the prison and indeed in the world outside, not to mention his own family. Now he reacted strongly: 'In that case there ought to be the fullest inquiry into the case. If on both her father's and mother's side and among her own sisters there is a strain of imbecility and insanity, then most careful inquiry ought to be made before her sentence is confirmed. I most sincerely trust that she will be reprieved.'

Percy Wisbey, having laboured over his petition, begged the *Daily Mail* to hold a copy at their offices for signatures, since he was placed so far out of town. Gladly, the newspaper accepted the duplicate, to lie open until July 12th, when it would have to be forwarded to Whitehall. It was felt that, 'The *Daily Mail* could not refuse this duty, while marvelling that it was left to a newspaper to help in this way, through the inaction of all the humanitarian societies.'

Mrs MA Hull came forward to state to the *Daily Mail* that she and her husband were caretakers at the Manchester Street Board School from 1886 to 1893, and knew Mary Ann Ansell for over two years. She was the butt of the other children, who used to jeer at her, and throw things at her in the street, calling out, 'Silly Old Ansell!' One day, without any warning, she thrust her hand through a pane of glass on the Girls' staircase, and cut herself badly. When they asked her why she had done it, she would only say, 'I don't know.' Once she locked herself up with a nail and a piece of string in an outhouse. She said that she did not know why, and looked vacant. Although she did not appear to be vicious, she would suddenly throw anything handy at the other children and then stand and laugh in a silly way. They were convinced that Mary Ann was not, while they knew her, a sane person.

Mrs Mary Sage, of 19 Manchester Street, where the Board School was situated, was troubled enough to write to the Home Office on July 8th, 'I wish to testify that one of the Ansells and I feel almost certain that it was Mary Ann, was in my service some years ago and I had to discharge her as she seemed intellectually unfit for the care of children. In fact almost all the time I had her I was frightened at what might be the result as moments of mental irresponsibility seemed to come over her and she could then hardly be accountable for her actions. I think a great injustice would be done if she is hanged.' This is exasperating; the alarming maid is very probably the convicted Mary Ann Ansell, but Mrs Sage's honest lack of certainty invalidates her information, which was minuted, 'not very positive'.

The Romilly Society, having for its objects, *inter alia*, the abolition of cruel punishments, and the prevention and redress of miscarriage of justice, which was obviously a natural enemy of the Home Office, received short shrift when Charles Henry Hopwood, QC, Liberal MP, who had founded the society in 1897, wrote from 1 Essex Court, Temple, approaching the case on public grounds and saying that it was believed that the execution of a young girl would cause a thrill of horror to pass through the country and stir up an unwholesome morbid feeling in her favour. It would produce strong and heated reflections upon circumstantial evidence, creating doubt and uncertainty in the public mind as to the correctness of the verdict and justice of the sentence. The Home Office, in the person of Charles Murdoch, unmoved by the rather different approach, took only one simpler point and noted that, 'It is a curious argument that if she be guilty the circumstances show such a depravity as will make people feel she is hardly accountable.' In the Home Office hierarchy, the Assistant Under-secretary who was dealing with the Ansell case was Charles Stewart Murdoch, CB (1838–1908), son of Sir Clinton Murdoch. He was Old School, and he was not a lawyer.

The Reverend Whyte Ayer, assistant curate of the Church of the Holy Cross, where all the Ansell children had been christened, wrote to say that, having known all the Ansell family for some years, he did not consider any of them to be of strong intellect. The girls in particular seemed to be the worst, as they soon developed the effects of scrofula. His letter was politely acknowledged and seen by the Home Secretary, but not by any medical man. Before the advent of antibiotics, scrofula, 'the King's Evil', was rife, a chronic invasion of the lymph nodes, especially of the neck, with unsightly, and later hideous swellings, the overlying skin turning a blueish purple, sometimes further disfigured by a sinus and an open wound. Tuberculosis was the common cause, but other mycobacteria could also have their effect. It used to be thought that there was an heredity element. Unpasteurized milk from infected cows was the main factor. There might have been an association with impaired intellect.

Margaret Bancroft, the American worker in the field, influential in the early twentieth century for her writings on Mental Subnormality, wrote of 'families where insanity, feeble-mindedness, scrofula, tuberculosis, etc. have existed to such a degree as to be marked.... Under the hereditary caption we note also hydrocephalus or dropsy of the brain, frequently caused by scrofula or tumours pressing under the brain, and often developed before the child is born.'[21] Deprived children like the Ansells were a pitiful sight, running freely around the grimy streets, exhibiting the stigmata of this unpleasant disease.

Meanwhile, at home in Tankerton Street, on July 9th, Mary Ann's mother wrote a trusting letter to the Queen, and it was passed straight on to the Home Office. A supporter wrote it for her, in a flowing hand:

> To her Majesty The Queen Victoria of England I a broken hearted Mother beg mercy for my poor child now laying under sentence of death for the sake of me and my seven little children and losing one 7 years ago in an accident beg of you our Great Majesty to answer my humble prayer in the name of our Lord Jesus Christ and our great civerlizion [sic] and our Great Home Secretary in the name of our Lord I beg pardon From a broken hearted Mother I remain your most humble servant Sarah Ansell.

The Monarch did not hear her plea, and Charles Murdoch noted, 'No mention is made by the mother of any weakness of intellect.'

---

21 See *Collected Papers of Margaret Bancroft on Mental Subnormality and the Care and Training of Mentally Subnormal Children*, 1914, pp. 20-22.

Mary Ansell.
A caricature, intended to help her.

THE VICTIM.

LEAVESDEN ASYLUM.

THE CORONER.

DR. T. STEVENSON.

MISS NOAKES.

NURSE FELMINGHAM.

SUPT. WOOD. PRODUCES THE WRAPPER.

MARY ANSELL

THE PRISONER.

THE WATFORD POISONING CASE.

James Ansell,
Mary Ann's hard-working,
God-fearing father

Sarah Ansell, mother.
Woman of sorrows

Martha Ansell,
Mary Ann's sister,
before her removal to
Leavesden Asylum

Caroline Ansell,
murder victim.
Not from life -
an imaginary drawing

Emma Ansell,
Mary Ann's sister,
and their father's prop,
with full literacy and
able to work

The Hampstead Heath railway tragedy

Crow Nest, Dewsbury, Yorkshire -
Mary Ann's previous place of employment

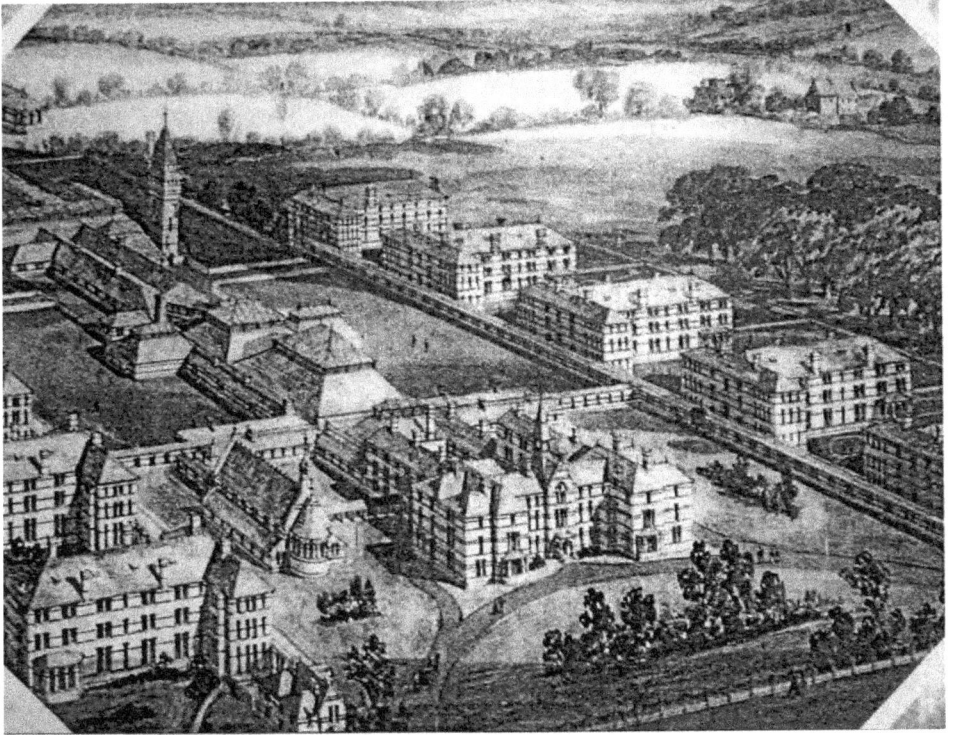

Leavesden Asylum in the countryside.
Architect's drawing from The Builder, 1868

A female ward at Leavesden Asylum, c.1900
from The Leavesden Hospital Story 1870-1995 by Kevin Brown

Mary Ann Ansell in the Police Court.
First drawing, and probably quite true-to-life

Superintendent William Wood,
who suspected Mary Ann from the first

Sir Matthew White Ridley,
Home Secretary

William Clarke Hall, Mary Ann's barrister
© National Portrait Gallery, London

Dr. Forbes Winslow
Defender of the Insane

Dr. Forbes Winslow
meets the hangman

Mr Berry (to Dr Forbes Winslow): "You've always got something to say."

˙ MARY ANSELL'S GRANDMOTHER
(Who, through being shut in a dark room while a child, was rendered weak-minded and subject to fits throughout her life).

MARY ANSELL'S FATHER
(Married a woman whose two aunts died mad in asylum).

CAROLINE	MARY ANNE	A boy	MARTHA	Four
(Four years in Leavesden Asylum for Imbeciles, until her death through the poisoned cake).	(Now under sentence of death).	who died young through an accident.	(A girl of sixteen who is a hopeless imbecile).	other young children.

Unusual 'Geneaological Table'
provided by the Daily Mail, 7th July 1899

Sixième année — N° 147   Huit pages : CINQ centimes   Dimanche 30 Juillet 1899

Le Petit Parisien

SUPPLÉMENT LITTÉRAIRE ILLUSTRÉ

Tous les jours
Le Petit Parisien
5 centimes

DIRECTION: 18, rue d'Enghien, PARIS

Tous les jeudis
SUPPLÉMENT LITTÉRAIRE
5 centimes

UNE FEMME PENDUE EN ANGLETERRE
EXÉCUTION DE L'EMPOISONNEUSE MARY ANSELL

CHAPTER EIGHT

MOTIVE IN HER MADNESS

There were nine days left, and Percy Wisbey decided to intensify his approach. It is doubtful that there was any money left in the purse, but his next series of endeavours were going to be more expensive than he had ever imagined when he agreed to take on the unpromising case. On Monday, June 19th, dressed particularly smartly, he boarded the train for Town and made his way to 33 Devonshire Street, in the West End, for an appointment with Dr Forbes Winslow. He had never done anything like this before, but the doctor will have been urbane and reassuring, although surprised by the youth of this provincial solicitor with his intolerable burden and gravely in need of a strong, authoritative figure to support him in his lonely plight.

Dr Lyttleton Stewart Forbes Winslow (1844-1913) was the people's defender in the criminal courts when there was an issue of insanity, and he was a household name, but not, in fact, unknown to Percy Wisbey, the best choice for the task of saving Mary Ann Ansell.[22] The young lawyer turned to him in all innocence, not understanding the background. The reality was that the Establishment was prejudiced against him, and Mary Ann was firmly in the clutches of the Home Office. A more respected alienist with no history of unfortunate incidents would have been more likely to have the ear of the Secretary of State. It was Forbes Winslow's own fault that he had lost the confidence of the Courts. He had serious quirks of

---

22 The doctor's own account of the Ansell case appears in his *Recollections of Forty Years* (1910) pp. 191-199.

character. He was convinced that every prisoner hopefully brought to his attention by the defence was in fact insane. This was his undoing in the Amelia Dyer baby farming trial of 1896, where it was only too obvious that her motive was pure gain and that she was feigning madness. He caused amusement when he thought that he had revealed the identity of Jack the Ripper and proudly displayed his supposed boots. Even so, he was, like his father Dr Benignus Forbes Winslow, a passionate defender of the insane criminal and a very experienced doctor. He particularly abhorred the hanging of women, regarding them as frail vessels, swayed by their emotions.

There was another, extreme problem: Forbes Winslow himself knew perfectly well that, after sentence of death, a new, outside, medical man, not appointed by the Home Office, was not permitted to see the prisoner, by virtue of inflexible rules. As he put it, 'The Government, in cases where no plea of insanity has been raised at the trial, refuse to allow outside interference. They and their medical advisers are alone the judges of whether certain questions raised after conviction are sufficient to justify a reprieve on the ground of insanity.' He complained that he had been called in too late on a number of occasions. He did not communicate this situation to Percy Wisbey during their consultation. Nevertheless, on that same day, he sent a typewritten letter to the Home Office asking for the necessary permit to interview Mary Ann Ansell, having been approached by the defending solicitor. This apparently straightforward request was a kind of bluff; he knew what the answer would be. Percy Wisbey, in good faith, filled with hope, sent a letter, similarly typewritten, to the Home Office: 'It is desirable inasmuch that I am instructed that she [MAA] is of unsound mind that she should be at once medically examined and I should be obliged therefore if you would kindly send me an order to permit Dr Forbes Winslow of London to see her at the Prison for that purpose.'

'Decline,' Charles Murdoch wrote briefly, and a letter to that effect was sent. The Secretary of State had, meanwhile, ordered that Mr Percy Wisbey should be asked to submit his petition *as soon as possible* [underlined] by return of post if practicable. This he did, appending two affidavits,[23] and his covering letter stated plaintively, 'I had intended to add an affidavit by Dr Forbes Winslow but as he is declined permission to examine the convict I am of course unable to do so.' He also said that, 'There are, I believe, two or three petitions being extensively signed by the Public praying for a reprieve and these will I understand reach you almost immediately.'

The Wisbey petition was impeccably presented. He put forward his own opinion, based on his several long conversations with the prisoner, that her mental capacity was to great degree deficient, based upon her demeanour and her apparent absolute incapacity to realize the serious nature of her position. Secondly, Caroline Ansell was an imbecile at the time of her death. Thirdly, 'Your petitioner has made enquiries and he is informed and verily believes that a younger sister of the Prisoner named Martha Ansell is also well known to be insane, and that application has been made to admit her to the Leavesden Asylum for Imbeciles.'

Fourthly, 'Your petitioner is further informed and verily believes that the paternal grandmother of the prisoner was subject to epileptic fits to such an extent as to amount to insanity, and that her great aunts on her mother's side both died imbecile in lunatic Asylums where they had both been confined for many years.' Further points were the extreme youth, 22 years of age; the almost entire absence of motive, which 'in opinion of your petitioner indicates a species of moral paralysis.'

Margaret Molony swore in her accompanying affidavit that Mary Ann Ansell was, from the start of her employment 'of sullen morose disposition and that at times she would mumble to herself and laugh or cry in a violent manner for no cause whatever at times.' During the last year, 'the said symptoms were more pronounced and in addition she became a victim to hallucinations at frequent

---

23 The pair of Molony affidavits cover the same ground as their published letters to the *Daily Mail*, in shorter form. They have stuck to their guns and not softened their points. It is slightly unfortunate that the pages do not spell their names correctly, written as Malony, while the signatures on the same page appear clearly as Molony. They were sworn locally, at 28 Great James Street, Bedford Row, on July 10th, and the surname of the Commissioner of Oaths was 'Box'.

intervals, constant weeping fits, and became spiteful positively to all persons and animals alike. I say that from these symptoms and my personal knowledge of the said Mary Ann Ansell it is my firm conviction and belief that she is a person of unsound mind to a great degree and sufficiently so as to be irresponsible for her actions.' At last, a whisper of *McNaughton*, but unfortunately from the wrong person.[24]

Crippled by the conspicuous lack of medical opinion, the petition contains nothing new and is unimpressive as to substance. The combination of the prohibition of Dr Forbes Winslow's attendance, (which was inevitable) and the demand for immediate production of the petition, has left Percy Wisbey no opportunity to regroup and at least to get in a written opinion from Dr Forbes Winslow, or, indeed, from any other medical authority. Wisbey's inexperience must be a factor here. The Home Office thought little of the petition, and a possible escape route for Mary Ann was sealed:

> This of course is a new line of defence the plea at the trial being innocence.
>
> Insanity in the family is alleged but no evidence in support of the statement is forwarded.
>
> The solicitor adverts to her extraordinary demeanour at the trial and to her incapability of realizing the serious nature of her position.
>
> This is contrary to the opinion of the learned judge who thought she behaved with much shrewdness in giving her evidence.
>
> There is no request for further medical enquiry. In view of these representations and those contained in the newspaper which certainly are for the most part mere hearsay evidence and the fact that no doubt every attempt will be made to make capital out of the refusal to allow Dr Winslow (sic) to see her – see marked passage in *Daily Mail* Extract I think it would be more satisfactory that Dr Nicolson and Dr Brayn should examine her.

This deliberation was the work of Charles Murdoch, dated July 12th. Kenelm Digby added a note, 'I agree but I should like to discuss

---

24 The McNaughton Rules (1843) formulated by the judges, defined legal insanity. Dr Forbes Winslow's father, Benignus, had a historical connection with the matter. Dr Forbes Winslow himself provides the pith of the Rules for the edification of the Home Office in his last letter to that office before the execution (see Chapter Nine).

this with you.' The Secretary of State himself, on the same day, wrote finally, 'I think Dr Nicolson and Dr Brayn should examine her.'

There is something very distasteful about the idea of 'making capital'; the thought expressed here is not rooted in a common desire for justice. The objection to the lack of evidence as to hereditary insanity is unfair. The Home Office knew that the defence had been operating on a low budget, and, for all that they knew, the petition was being prepared totally *gratis*. Dr Forbes Winslow liked to be paid for consultations and used to grumble that instructing solicitors rarely came back to him with a fee; it seems doubtful that he was going to be paid for what he had already done to advise Percy Wisbey, or for his later work on the case. If he had had more time, resources and experience, Percy Wisbey could have tried to obtain a record of the two aunts' admissions, that is if Mary Ann's parents could have named the holding hospitals. Their sense of shame could have been overcome. He never ventured to Tankerton Street, as a modern criminal solicitor would have done, or at least sent a clerk. He did not approach the St Pancras Poor Law Relieving Officer, the Duly Authorised Officer, predecessor of the Mental Welfare Officer, who knew the family and could have held useful records. There was no way of proving the epileptic insanity of the paternal grandmother who seemed to have survived at home, unless knowledge of her admissions had been purposively withheld.

As a matter of fact, there was a way of tracing good, documentary evidence of the insanity of a family member. Unexpectedly, this was Harriett Parish, Mary Ann's first cousin, in whose name a false letter had been written to Caroline. Percy Wisbey knew nothing about this matter. Earlier, on April 10th, when the police were known to be searching for Harriett, two letters written by an informant named Elizabeth Bennet were received at the Home Office, sent on from the Hertfordshire Chief Constable. Their significance appears not to have been appreciated. Very difficult to decipher, written in a sprawling Board School hand, and rambling in content, they do actually repay close scrutiny.

Headed, 54 Oxford Street, Whitstable [Kent] the first letter states:

> Sir, on reading the account of the death sentence on Mary Ansell in Lloyds I remembered some years ago a woman named Harriett Parish who was a patient in Wandsworth Asylum Surrey at the time I was detained there as a patient I remember also that Caroline Ansell the poisoned woman was also at Wandsworth at the same time these patients both Ansell with Parish having both been removed to Leavesden or Parish may have had her discharge. You might make some inquiries about this as sometimes there is ill feeling between these patients and these inquiries might result in something. I do not know at what time Parish left. Doctors by referring to their account books might tell you. Yrs truly Elizabeth Bennet PS this was the name on the cake Harriett Parish.

The second letter covers the same points, with some added detail, viz: 'these patients walked in the same grounds Harriett Parish being more sane than C Ansell', and, 'Parish was a fine-built woman.'

These letters may explain why Caroline was so trusting in her reaction to the false letter, if her relationship with Harriett Parish was closer than mere kin. This is the only known reference to Caroline Ansell's previous admission to Wandsworth Asylum, later named Springfield Hospital. She could of course have been another girl by that same name. Even Elizabeth Bennet is aware that asylum records are there to be used. If only Mary Ann Ansell herself had walked in those grounds, this story could have been different indeed. It was Charles Murdoch who assessed the Bennet letters and did not refer them upwards: 'Letters from a former patient in an Asylum. Nothing material in them.'

The opinion of Mr Justice Mathew that Mary Ann Ansell had exhibited *much shrewdness* was a nail in her coffin. It is remarkably strange, however, that Dr Forbes Winslow, who had no means of knowing that the judge would be signalling with this non-legal, non-psychiatric term, had already let it be known that, 'Her clear, shrewd answers were, in his opinion, distinct symptoms of insanity.' What he meant was that her manner was removed from reality, as if the events were not happening to her. Later doctors would say that her 'affect' was inappropriate.

Locked in her cell at St Albans, Mary Ann's condition was 'most pitiable'. Her mother was allowed to see her for ten minutes on

Monday, July 10th, and found her pale and thin. She could scarcely speak, and stared at her mother with glassy eyes as if she could not recognise her. 'I am sure the poor thing didn't know where she was or what she was doing,' said Sarah Ansell. 'Her weak mind is worse now.'

The *Daily Mail* of July 11th carried an interview with a disillusioned Percy Wisbey with some remarks which he would surely have preferred to keep private, but it did not really seem to matter now.

> "In many minds," [he said] "there is a feeling that, but for the very strong line taken by Mr Justice Mathew in his summing-up, the jury would, at any rate, not have agreed to the verdict which they actually returned …"
>
> Mr Wisbey has decided not to suggest in the petition that the judge unduly emphasised the case against the girl, inasmuch as the Home Secretary will, in the ordinary course of things, send the petition to the judge for his opinion.

Hopefully, on July 13th, the same newspaper commented that the evidence collected since the trial was more likely to carry conviction than any lists of names on petitions: the document at the *Daily Mail* office had attracted some 500 signatures. Neither 'hearsay' nor petitions were in fact having any effect at all on the Home Office, as shown by the ongoing private commentary of those assisting the Secretary of State. However, the *Daily Mail*, unaware of the strength of the opposition of the Government, carried on robustly, arguing that by allowing affidavits of Mary Ann Ansell's mental unsoundness to be placed before him, 'the Home Secretary has shown that he is not in agreement with those who think the plea for insanity should not be raised at all if it was not put forward at the trial.

'Such an argument might apply in the case of a prisoner with sufficient funds to command an elaborate and exhaustive defence, but in Mary Ansell's case the evidence which the *Daily Mail* has since unearthed was unknown to counsel briefed for the defence. Investigations into the girl's past career could not be made without expense, and the purse of this wretched imbecile servant girl was something less than slender.'

It was not customary for counsel to comment on their cases, and Clarke Hall had withdrawn, but Percy Wisbey was turning the truths over in his mind, and speaking out in his own defence, not mentioning financial problems. The *Hertfordshire Advertiser* called on him for answers on Thursday, 13th July, and elicited an explanation:

> The question of insanity was not raised at the time of the trial, for the simple reason that it could not be. When you are defending a person you have naturally to take his or her instructions and it ought to be patent to everyone that the accused does not want to plead insanity and be sent to Broadmoor straight away, even assuming that we could have convinced the jury that she was not in a fit state to plead. And then, supposing we could not have convinced the jury, she would have been hung [*sic*] straight away, because there would have been no other defence left. Of course, where a man is caught in the act of murdering his children the only defence is insanity.

We do not need to be too impressed by the standard of these excuses. The argument about not wanting to go to Broadmoor straight away applies only to non capital cases. Better life in the lunatic wards than death in the hanging shed. The risk of conviction and execution after a weak fight against strong evidence was far, far higher than the risk of failing in a well-prepared plea of insanity supported by expert medical evidence, preferably not emanating from Dr Forbes Winslow. The young solicitor said now that he knew, of course, that Caroline had been in Leavesden Asylum, and he knew that application had been made for the admission of another sister, but he had not known about the two aunts and the grandmother. This is a disgraceful admission, at a time, too, when a whole phalanx of 'lunatics' standing behind and beside you would buttress your plea remarkably. However, he continued defiantly, even if he had known about them, he would not have brought forward a plea of insanity.

Seeing no contradiction in his stance, as he rationalised it, he related how he had gone to see Dr Forbes Winslow, 'the famous specialist, who, I may remark, has taken a deep interest in this case, and had a long talk with him. He expressed the opinion that the prisoner must be mad.' Asked if he thought that the refusal to allow Dr Forbes Winslow to examine Mary Ann Ansell was not a little hard, he agreed: 'Yes, because Dr Forbes Winslow is such a well-known man that his opinion could be relied upon as absolutely fair and unbiased...his opinion (either way) would have been of great value.' Since the official refusal, he had instructed the doctor to report on the full facts of the case as laid before him, and he would then despatch it by express messenger to the Home Secretary.

The journalist asked Wisbey if he had discovered why the application had not been granted. It was a good question: this is just the kind of vital knowledge that a young lawyer is not taught and has to find out for himself. 'I have made enquiries,' he said, 'and am told that it is contrary to the custom of the Home Office to allow any mental expert to examine a prisoner after conviction, except he be nominated and associated with the Treasury, or connected with the prison where the condemned person is confined. Before the trial every facility is given for an independent examination, but after conviction the doors are shut to any outside interference.' If only he had known this before! 'There is no doubt that if the prisoner is hung [sic] a serious question will be raised as to why Dr Forbes Winslow was not allowed to see her. For that matter it is contrary to custom to allow the defending solicitor to see the prisoner after conviction, but if the regulation can be withdrawn in his case [and he was certainly allowed access to Mary Ann] there is no earthly reason why the same latitude cannot be allowed in the case of a doctor.'

These words prove that Dr Forbes Winslow had not seen fit to tell Wisbey in person that he would not be allowed into St Albans gaol. He had allowed Wisbey to write artlessly for a pass for him, and, playing along, had made the same request on his own behalf. Anxious not to appear in a poor light with the Home Office, the doctor proceeded on July 12th to write them a weaselly letter:

> I beg to thank you for your letter received...I had informed those who had instructed me that it was contrary to the custom of your Office to allow Doctors, except nominated by the Treasury or connected with the Prison, to examine and report upon condemned

persons. I have this morning received instructions from the Solicitor, who is conducting the defence, to forward to him a report upon the whole history of the case. I have avoided going into the matter before, as I wanted to have an open mind in the event of the precedent being departed from. My report will be forwarded to you by the Solicitor together with the petition in the usual way.

Percy Wisbey told the reporter that he understood that a doctor *would* be making an examination [for the Home Office], probably Dr Savage, who did a great deal of work for the Treasury. Dr George Henry Savage (1842-1921) knighted in 1912, would have been an eminent man for the Crown to call upon. He held posts which included Physician Superintendent of Bethlem Royal Hospital, Consulting Physician to Guy's Hospital, and, of particular relevance, to Earlswood Idiot Asylum. He was President of the Medico-Psychological Association of Great Britain and of the Neurological Society. His town address was 26 Devonshire Place, near Dr Forbes Winslow. As he grew older, he concentrated on consultancy. Most famously, no doubt, he had the anxious care of Virginia Woolf during her cyclothymic episodes, and she grew to dread his regime for her of strict bed rest and deprivation of reading and writing. At Bethlem, he had favoured some restraint. Called in by the Home Office in 1890, he would not save Mary Eleanor Pearcey – who wheeled a perambulator loaded with the bodies of her love-rival and her baby through the streets of North London – although she was an epileptic with 'absences'. This was one of the murder cases where Dr Forbes Winslow was consulted too late and his written report was not effective. It was Dr Savage who opposed Dr Forbes Winslow in the previously mentioned Dyer baby farmer trial where, his services paid for, unusually, as he said, by the Treasury, Dr Forbes Winslow conspicuously failed to establish her insanity.

If Percy Wisbey had not been an opponent of capital punishment before he had become involved in this most difficult of cases, he certainly was now:

It is a remarkable thing that when a case of this kind occurs there are hundreds of people ready to come forward and sign petitions on behalf of the prisoner, not because they believe in the prisoner's innocence, but because they object to capital punishment on principle. Such a method of action is absurd. What they should do is to get their member to introduce a Bill in Parliament for the abolition of capital punishment. I have had a mass of correspondence on the subject from people raising all sorts of questions. Many want to know why the insurance agent isn't prosecuted. It is no doubt a crying scandal that insurance agents should dun poor people like they do to insure their relatives.

On this note, the long interview recorded in the *Hertfordshire Advertiser* came to a conclusion.

Even before the solicitor's approach to him, Dr Forbes Winslow had been eagerly perusing the press reports and interviews, with drawings of Mary Ann, and had felt the crusader's fire which stirred inside him when he sensed an injustice to an insane person. On July 12th, the *Daily Mail* had already published a preliminary shot: 'An eminent insanity specialist, Dr Forbes Winslow declares:- I have no hesitation in saying that the evidence throughout the case, the facts which have been made public concerning the family, and the story of the prisoner's behaviour told by Mr and Mrs Maloney [*sic*], all point to the conclusion that the girl is a mental degenerate, irresponsible for her action in causing her sister's death.'

On July 13th, the Home Office received the doctor's official report. Courteously typewritten for clarity and impact, it still has an erratic appearance:

> 1st. HEREDITY. Of this there is not the slightest doubt. She is a mental degenerate so often seen in Families where Insanity exists, as in hers, to any great extent. Such an individual is allowed her freedom being simply regarded by her Family and neighbours as a weak minded poor fool, but harmless and there being nothing objective in her condition, she is not like her Sister incarcerated in a Lunatic Asylum. There are two insane Sisters, and insanity inherited both on the Father's and Mother's side.
>
> 2nd. MOTIVE. There is generally "method in madness" and often motive is an act of insanity. I think that too much [h]as been laid on the insurance policy for £11. At the time she was contemplating the deed very possibly some insane idea was passing thro her so called mind.
>
> 3rd. BEHAVIOUR DURING TRIAL. This is in my opinion most

important. There was an absence of excitement or emotion during the whole proceedings, and an inability to realise her condition or the gravity of the act. The summing up of the judge and sentence of death did not in any way affect her. This is most unusual even in the hardened Criminals.

4th. INDICATIONS OF INSANITY. Intense passion and love alternating with each other. Frequent attacks of mental vacancy. Talking to herself in an incoherent manner, strange hallucinations, loud fits of laughter for no reason. Taciturnity, which frequently was for days, declining to speak to anyone. Imaginary grievances. Cruelty to her little Sisters, this symptom is often present in this class of Degenerate. Imaginary quarrels with persons not present, and she evdiently [sic] suffered from Hallucinations of hearing so often found in Criminal Homicidal Lunatics. All these symptoms without enumerating others are in themselves evidence of a disordered mind.

I am of opinion that if the question of her Insanity had been raised at the Trial that no jury could have convicted her upon the evidence which might have been adduced. In order for a person to be legally responsible she would be supposed to know the difference between right and wrong and the nature and gravity of the act committed by her.

That she did not know this difference I have not the slightest doubt, this is quite confirmed by what the Chaplain of the Prison has stated "THAT SHE CAN'T BE MADE TO UNDERSTAND WHAT MURDER IS" … If a person commits a murder and at the time is unable to distinguish between right and wrong, be the crime ever so revolting, by the law of our Country that person is not a responsible individual.

I state, without fear of contradiction, that Mary Ansell would come under the category of persons unable to so discriminate, and I am of opinion that if the question of her being able to plead had been raised at the commencement of the Trial, and the fact had been placed before the Jury that she could not distinguish between right and wrong, that she would not have stood in the position we find her today, regarded as a responsible person with a complete knowledge of her acts and as such to undergo the full penalty of the law.

Forbes Winslow
MB, DCL,LLD.

This strong and persistent argument, compiled under pressure of time, making use, as it should have done, of the McNaughton Rules which defined insanity for the courts, was vitiated by Charles Murdoch's 'mere hearsay' without access to the prisoner. Even so his findings would not have been dissimilar if he had been in close contact with her, when she would have fitted into the substance of all the experience of his years of running the family private asylums. The report appeared in the *Daily Mail*, annoyingly breaching its confidential aspect, as far as the Home Office was concerned, and it was included verbatim in the doctor's *Recollections of Forty Years* (1910), where there was an additional report, not intended for the Home Office:

> Mary Ansell's portrait, together with those of her father, mother, and sisters were submitted to me:- "A typical specimen of a mental degenerate of the lowest order. The whole features point to a condition of irresponsibility. I should think that, in addition to the irresponsibility, there must have been a moral perversion. Our county asylums contain many of these persons similarly afflicted. I should think, judging from the formation of the head and face, that there is absolutely no power of mental concentration or of analysing in her mind the nature of any act she might contemplate committing.
>
> "Her whole type appears to be between a criminal and a lunatic, but one where the criminal line has been overstepped and the lunatic mind developed. Insanity, passion, and crime are so closely connected, that it is a very difficult matter to know where one begins and the other ends. From the description I have received of the unfortunate girl, I consider this to be a very good likeness, and illustrates the type of degenerates to which she belongs. With regard to Mary Ansell's hand [a drawing is provided, howsoever acquired], there is an absence of any marked head-line, and the weak and indistinct finger form and the general indecision of character are to be observed."

A summation reads: 'Mary Ansell was a woman of a very weak mind. Her appearance was that of an imbecile.'

Back in 1899, all of those who were relying upon the effect of Dr Forbes Winslow's report would have been amazed beyond all measure if they could have had sight of the derisive reaction at the Home Office: '*Dr Winslow's opinion is not entitled to much weight – but the Examining Doctors may as well see it.*' (Author's italics)

Charles Murdoch is the signatory, and Kenelm Digby initialled the minute.

The *Daily Mail* petition – i.e. the duplicate prepared by Percy Wisbey

– also arrived at the Home Office on July 13th, and was similarly disregarded: 'Practically the same as the previous only there is no reference to the affidavits of prisoner's late employers. On the ground of insanity in the family and herself unsupported by any evidence as to how they obtained the information about the family history. Said this to Dr Brayn to whom papers went yesterday.' (Charles Murdoch and Kenelm Digby as above.) Briefing the two selected doctors of final reference was the matter most occupying the official mind. They were both Broadmoor men, although that was not mandatory, and therefore they were going to be seen as on the inside, since Broadmoor was under the jurisdiction of the Home Secretary. Would they let her in, as one of their own, or would they throw her to the wolves? Dr David Nicolson, CB, had been Superintendent there until 1895, when he retired and took up the less onerous and sought-after position of one of the Lord Chancellor's Visitors in Lunacy. Dr Richard Brayn (knighted in 1911) had taken over from Dr Nicolson in 1896, and was to stay in post until 1910. He had had a long career as Medical Officer and Governor in the prison service.

The first incumbent, Dr Meyer, suffered an attack by an inmate armed with a favourite weapon, a stone concealed in a handkerchief, while attending Holy Communion in the asylum chapel, and survived for only four years.[25] Dr Orange, his successor, was better known, because of his encouragement of Richard Dadd, the magical, mad artist: he, too, was attacked by the same modus, and had to retire after four years. Dr Nicolson came next, as number three. As Deputy Superintendent, he, too, had been felled while on his ward rounds and had been convalescent for six months and, as Superintendent, another attack left him concussed for ten weeks, but he persevered with his career, not surprisingly nostalgic for the good old days when 'mechanical restraint' was not regarded as beyond the pale. He introduced few changes, the best, perhaps, the photographing of all inmates for identification in the event of escape. He was 'always

---

25 The colourful anecdotage and characterisation of Drs Meyer and Nicolson can be found in Ralph Partridge's respected work, *Broadmoor: A History of Criminal Lunacy and its Problems* (1953), pp. 83-95.

more concerned to keep his patients in than to let them out.'

Reports by the Commissioners in Lunacy on Dr Nicolson's regime 'cannot have been entirely favourable. It is said that signs of slackness were observed among the medical officers in the performance of their duties. At any rate, when the time came to replace the Superintendent, it was decided to install a martinet.' This was Dr Brayn, 'the first of the "men of iron" who ruled Broadmoor for a generation.' He felt at home with criminals and the fact that his new subjects were mad as well made little difference. By no stretch of the imagination could he have been described as a distinguished alienist, with his authoritarian mind and inflexible discipline. No one ever escaped over the side of his tight ship. He was not brutal, but severe, limiting outside exercise and 'secluding' the troublesome inmates in small locked rooms 'with shutters closed and no gratings for air.' In 1899, the Visitors in Lunacy begged the Home Secretary for a reconsideration of this policy but in 1900 the recorded hours of seclusion rose to 200,000. Richard Dadd would not have thrived under his reign.

So, these were the two arbiters who were, in effect, to decide if Mary Ann Ansell lived or died. On the face of it, the present incumbent of Broadmoor, and his predecessor, potentially her keepers, were a fair and appropriate choice, but the reality was that Dr Nicolson was a weakened and probably cynical survivor, while his colleague, engaged in his personal battle to control Broadmoor, would seem to have been without pity in his zeal. Once again, Mary Ann had been unlucky in the men chosen to shepherd her through the last stages of her life. The doctors' job was not to be merciful – that was for the Home Secretary. They had given satisfaction before; Sir Matthew specified them by name, with a helpful note of Dr Nicolson's address – Clifton House, Guildford.

Entrusted, then, with their mission, the two experts travelled to St Albans where they interviewed her twice, on July 13th and 14th, in a proper room, not in her spartan cell, and Dr Brayn wrote up their joint report, for speed:

During our examination of the convict, we found no indication of insanity, and we have no reason to believe that at the time she accomplished her sister's death by means of poison she was otherwise than sane and responsible for her actions.

Mary Ann Ansell is 22 years of age, with features of a heavy and somewhat low type. She has, however, had a fair education and is fond of reading: in intelligence she is quite up to the average of her class,[26] and is in no sense the imbecile that she has sometimes been represented to be.

She gave us a circumstantial account of the events of her past life, and although in the first instance she denied her guilt with regard to the murder, she ultimately confessed that she insured her sister's life with the express object of obtaining the insurance money: having in her mind at the time the intention of possibly taking her sister's life with a view to realizing the money speedily, in order to facilitate arrangements for her own marriage.

She admits that in February she attempted to poison her sister with Oxalic Acid, which she mixed with the sugar sent to the Asylum in a parcel with some tea, and that she endeavoured to avert suspicion by writing the letter signed "Harriett Parish", telling her sister that her parents were dead. She further admitted that in March, with the intention of poisoning her sister, she sent her the portion of cake in which she had placed the phosphorus paste which was proved to have caused her death.

Throughout our conversations with Mary Ann Ansell she was perfectly rational; she answered all our questions intelligently, and showed herself quite capable of appreciating the nature and import of the points raised by us, and of realizing the gravity of her position.

Although some evidence of insanity in the family has been produced, she informed us that she herself had never been insane, and we were unable to detect in her the existence of any delusion, hallucination, or other indication of mental disease.

We have to add that the prisoner informed us that she selected her sister Caroline's life for insurance because, being in the Asylum, she was "out of the way", and her death might be accomplished with less risk of detection.

The Matron of the Prison who is an experienced and intelligent officer, and who has had the prisoner constantly under observation during the past three months, informed us that she (the prisoner) had not exhibited any symptoms of insanity, and the Chairman of the Visiting Committee, and the Governor, and the Medical Officer of the Prison, whom we saw, concurred in this view.

26 An unscientific comment, coming from doctors on the threshold of the twentieth century.

The report was a confidential document, kept secret from the public, who had no idea of the contents, especially the confession, and it was a virtual death warrant. With this screed before them, the Home Office dug into their already entrenched position.

The convict condemned to death, but, crucially, hoping for a reprieve, had no legal rights, and it may well seem wrong to a later generation that Mary Ann was placed in a situation where she made a full confession with no legal adviser to protect her. There is no evidence that the two alienists pressed or manoevred her into an intention or desire to confess, but they certainly asked her what had happened. They were honour-bound, one would presume, to reveal to her that they were acting for the State, but it is only too possible to imagine that she did not understand the significance of the interviews. Removed from her cell to a more comfortable room, with a couple of kind and genial doctors, there just for her, when she had always been taught that doctors were beneficent, she was intensely vulnerable and alone. It does not seem to have been in her nature to desire to please, but she might have thought that she had done rather well, as she was hurried back to her cell.

The oxalic acid was a great surprise. It intensified the premeditation, but does not make her doubly wicked. This poison, also known as sorrel, or salts of sorrel, which occurs in rhubarb leaves, could have been in any kitchen, as a cleaning agent, and was as easily available for purchase as phosphorus. There was no suggestion of it in the prosecution case; everyone was misled by the neat way in which demerara sugar could conceal yellow phosphorus. Both poisons can cause a very painful death. Are we to think that oxalic acid was Mary Ann's first choice, but she abandoned it when the tea and sugar bait failed, and turned then to phosphorus, experimenting with it in three or four bottles? The blunt assertion that she was of average intelligence was very damaging, because with insanity ruled out by Drs Nicolson and Brayn, only impaired intellect was left to mitigate. They certainly ought to have recognised mental defect, since, in that precise year, 1899, ninety-nine 'imbeciles' were tabled at Broadmoor. If she had been really cunning, and had understood all the issues relating to her suitability for a reprieve, she would have feigned insanity in front of all the prison, and Broadmoor, authorities. The all-important motive of funds for marriage which was imputed to her, was, in fact vitiated by the circumstance that she had already taken a room, equipped it, and bought a wedding dress.

Too little was made, too late, of the unfortunately hearsay evidence of the rejecting behaviour of the young man when she presented herself to him as a bride. This was a Miss Havisham moment with a catastrophic potential. She might have reasoned that Caroline's 'imbecile' status was an impediment to her own marriage, and that she would have been no worse for elimination.

In the view of the judges, a concrete, understandable motive which could be labelled 'vengeance' or 'financial gain' was utterly damning and outweighed any highfaluting psychological twaddle.

The uncertainty attached to the exact nature of Mary Ann's mental status was a strong factor in the failure to save her. The Home Office was determined to portray her as perfectly normal but the general public saw her as 'weak-minded'. It did not help that Dr Forbes Winslow, confusingly, as if hedging his bets, put forward three diagnoses: moral insanity, lunacy, and mental defectiveness. There was more low intelligence and epilepsy than insanity in the living Ansell family and its forbears, and this caused uncertainty. There were so many Mary Ann Ansells: the father's sensible daughter; the judge's shrewd criminal; the chaplain's dull, uncomprehending girl; the jury's insane offender; the gatekeeper's unhinged person; the Molonys', teachers' and caretakers' mentally deficient outcast.

Heredity disposition was of paramount relevance to the psychiatrists, but, as Dr Forbes Winslow complained, disregarded by the judges. Mr Justice Wright's jibe[27] that a grandmother's niece's insanity did not prove that Charles Maidment was out of his mind, illustrates the judicial hostility. Presumably there was a chromosomal defect in the Ansell family line. The drawings made for Dr Forbes Winslow and published for the whole world to see,

27 v. page 127.

to save Mary Ann from the gallows, embody the idea of the 'taint'. It was hard for the parents to be depicted as of 'low type', and the third young daughter, presumably Emma, aged 14, is made to look like an idiot child, which she certainly was not. It was nearly worth it, because the pictured defect made many people feel uncomfortable about hanging Mary Ann. In the twentieth century when IQ testing was formalised, she would probably have been assessed as of borderline intelligence. Epilepsy might have followed. Historically, those of unsound or impaired mind were supposed to be exempt from hanging.

Also on the 13th, anticipating the worst, James and Sarah Ansell enlisted someone to write a most humble letter on their behalf to the Secretary of State:

> Sir will you kindly give me permission to receive my daughter Mary Ann Ansell now lying under sentence at St Albans prison her cape and hat when we visit her next tuesday July 18th we should feel greatly greatly oblige to you we remain Sir your obedient servants J and S ansell Sir Matthew

The reaction of Charles Murdoch is frankly contemptible: *'They are evidently very ignorant people – but they do not say a word about insanity. All they want is the clothing of the wretched woman. To Prison Department to deal with.'* (Author's italics) He was evidently very ignorant of the plight of the very poor. The class divide could not be illustrated better than by these crass words. Mary's famous cape and hat certainly had resale value. The Ansells might, too, have thought that the public hangman was still permitted to take the prisoner's clothing for his own purposes, not realising that the right had been abolished in 1888.

Sir Matthew White Ridley has left posterity a written record of his final decision on one of the ordinary 'Minutes' sheets. What we do not have are notes of the oral discussions, mere conversations, and private debates, which, we would hope, were many and profound. It reads:

> I have seen the Judge and Drs Nicolson and Brayn. This was a most cold blooded and premeditated murder committed for the sake of

the insurance money on the life of the deceased, whom the prisoner insured for the very purpose.

There are no extenuating circumstances whatever.

The report of the Drs leaves no ground for holding the Prisoner insane or irresponsible for her actions.

As to age there is no precedent or reason for holding the comparatively youthful age of 22 a sufficient reason for respite.

There remains only the sex. Had a similar murder been committed by a man of 22, there would have been no doubt that the law should take its course. I think that sex alone should make no difference in such a case, and that to hold otherwise would practically be setting a precedent for the abolition of capital punishment in the case of women.

I am afraid the law must take its course.

MWR. July 15 1899

CHAPTER NINE

THE WISDOM OF JURORS

The Ansell family had been waiting at Tankerton Street. It was now Saturday, July 15th, and there had been no reply to Sarah's letter, pleading for her daughter's life. It was left to a *Sunday Times* reporter to tell them. When he called there to record their reaction to the Home Secretary's decision, he found that they did not know, so that he had to be the messenger. Sarah Ansell 'gave way to a pathetic outburst of wild grief,' while James controlled his emotions, saying that he had long hardened himself to bad news. Again and again, Sarah sobbed that Mary 'was silly from the time she went to school,' but James would not agree that she was insane. It was all like a nightmare to him, he said. The two sisters had always been on good terms and he could not bring himself to believe that Mary had plotted to kill Caroline. It seemed incredible to him, because he never heard a single word of malice. They had been led to believe that something would be done to help Mary. Hearing the commotion, neighbours gathered to commiserate with 'the old couple in their trouble.'

Mr Jobson, who had tried so hard to help, was told the news on that Saturday, when he received by post a personal letter from Charles Murdoch, for the Secretary of State, in relation to his petition with over one thousand signatures. On receiving it on July 13th, Murdoch had noted as his main response, 'The signatures seem entirely those of the lower classes.' Also on the 13th, a professionally drawn-up, formal petition came in from 'The Electors, Ratepayers and Inhabitants of the City of London' but it sank without trace. The signatories were mixed – doctors, actor, comedian, artist, engineer, housekeeper, nurse, cashier, clerk, salesman, agent, and so on.

Mr Jobson told the *Sunday Times* reporter that he felt quite overcome by the letter, which stated that insufficient grounds for reprieve had been found by the Home Secretary. He explained that he had taken up the case because he himself had suffered greatly through marrying into a family in which there was insanity. This had led him into studying the question, and, knowing Mary Ann personally, he had long known her to suffer from the family taint. (Mr Jobson was a watch-maker, and he did not reveal under what circumstances he had met Mary Ann.) He felt that the decision was deplorable, and he had expected a more merciful outcome. After the view expressed by Dr Forbes Winslow, he said, there had seemed to be every reason to expect a reprieve.

All parties, including newspapers such as the *Manchester Guardian* had been relying on Dr Forbes Winslow's opinion; he was not being criticised or being made fun of as he had been in Ripperian matters. He was still happy to talk to the press: 'I, of course, can hardly express an opinion on the Home Secretary's decision, as I have not seen the report which was presented him, but certainly I see no reason for altering my previous opinion, which was that Mary Ansell was absolutely insane.'

A letter to the *Daily Mail* from 'Disgusted' referred to the surprise and indignation felt by hundreds of people living in the Tankerton Street neighbourhood, and saying that, 'As I live very close to the street where the Ansell family reside, I may state that I know them very well by sight, and think that your efforts to place before the public the medical view of the "mental degeneracy" of Mary Ansell were very wisely directed.'

People of all types who had been touched by the case now had to face up to the reality of the outcome: family, neighbours, the Molonys, doctors and nurses at Leavesden, the insurance company and its agents, the purveyors of the poison, the clergy, the school staff, Mary Ann's lawyers, the jury, Mr Jobson, the handwriting expert, Dr Forbes Winslow, and those of the general public who did not want her to be hanged. Some suffered sleepless nights; they said so.

Many letters came in to the *Daily Mail*. The Home Office noted with satisfaction and exclamation marks that there was a discrepancy in the actual number counted. In one issue, they noted, one thousand, and then on the next page, ten thousand were claimed to have been received. Strong, ingenious, civilised, pleading, the selection of the letters ring with the old tragedy:

> I am one of the managers of the Metropolitan Asylums Board, and voted on Saturday last for the appeal for mercy, which was refused by the majority. I visited Leavesden Asylum when the inquiry was held there, and saw the father of the wretched girl. His appearance struck me as being more suitable for the asylum than many under our care, and I feel that the girl ought to receive the clemency of the Crown. (William F Penfold)

> The Home Secretary is a person of unquestionable humanity: but I cannot help thinking that he has been fettered in this instance by the regrettable action of the judge (also a merciful man in general), who, at the trial, gave the prisoner to understand that she need not look for human mercy. Such a remark seems unduly to prejudge the exercise of the sole, the Royal prerogative of mercy, and also in some degree to a [illegible] decision. Messrs Nicolson and Brayn are able experts, but they are not infallible. The family circumstances of the prisoner and her antecedents should have claimed full official consideration. For there is the gravest reason to apprehend that an insane person is about to be fatally punished for her disease. It is no part of my duties, as secretary of the Howard Association, to attempt to interfere with the operation of law in capital cases generally... I had confidently concluded that a commutation would be forthcoming, and am amazed and grieved at the Home Secretary's announcement. (William Tallack)

> The law allows the propagation of the mentally-unfit to go on unchecked. It sanctions an iniquitous system of insurance, but, with a cruel inconsistency, it punishes irrevocably the victims of its criminal laxity. The almost pathetic unattractiveness of this latest victim only seems to emphasise the national sense of horror at her unjust fate. We place side by side, by way of contrast, the two poisoning cases in

which Mrs Carew and Mary Ansell were respectively concerned. The more excusable of the two guilty women perishes! Surely there is one law for the rich – another for the poor. (Constance Clarke)

To hang a woman is an enormity. To hang an imbecile a crime. No jury will now convict a woman of murder. ('Mercy'. By telegram.)

Mary Ansell's crime was horrible. The decision which casts her into eternity in my opinion is more horrible...Still, there is one comforting reflection – after Wednesday next Mary Ansell will be of no further expense to the State. I have not computed the fraction of a farthing which her prolonged existence might have cost me. (Jas. S. Hayden)

Evidently a new organisation is required in "Darkest England" for not only is a Society for the Prevention of Cruelty to Animals and Children required but it is apparent that one for the Prevention of Cruelty to Lunatics should at once be established. (Charles Prescott)

When such a scoundrel as Prince is permitted to escape the gallows, to lead a comparatively easy life in a criminal asylum, and a poor lone girl, without money or influence, is made to pay the extreme penalty for an act of which she is mentally irresponsible, then England must indeed be losing her prestige for justice and mercy. (H. Hayward)

The question of life or death rests with one man... It seems incredible we allow such a state of things to exist. It is a national disgrace we have no court of criminal appeal. (DG Yeoman)

How in the face of the evidence produced since the trial Sir M White Ridley can have consented to this judicial murder is more than I can understand, and I can assure you that in this neighbourhood the feeling is one of consternation and horror, that he can have leant his name, a much-respected one, to such a damnable and barbarous decision. I am heart-sick and disgusted to know that any humane, sensible man, such as I know Sir MW Ridley to be, can have come to such a decision. (William L Phillips)

Must we now stand by helpless...? Would not some of her Majesty's faithful Commons join in petition to her Majesty? Her broad sense of justice and humanity, so often shown to her beloved people, would most assuredly direct a respite were but the mere facts laid before her. (Charles H Chapman)

⚜

Entirely agree with you regarding Mary Ansell. Hope possible direct appeal to her Majesty for new medical inquiry. (Rev Lord Archibald Douglas, by telegram)

⚜

This decision, in the face of the recent action of the Government in liberating the remaining members of the band of cowardly scoundrels who murdered in the most deliberate and bloodthirsty manner the victims of the Phoenix Park massacre, is certainly interesting, if for no other reason than that it appears wholly inexplicable.[28] Perhaps, however, an explanation may be afforded when it is remembered that the liberation of the Irish murderers may possibly influence a certain number of rebel votes in the House of Commons; while the judicial murder of Mary Ansell, poor miserable pauper that she is, is scarcely likely to affect the position of the Government, at any rate in the House, though its influence on the country is another matter. (F Grenfell Baker, MRCS)

⚜

It is the old, old story; one law for the poor, another for the rich. Note the contrast in the two sentences for a similar crime. Mary Ansell, poor, ignorant, uneducated, natural idiot, sentenced to death. Miss Peterson, well-to-do, cultured, well-educated, intelligent – sentenced to luxurious retirement during her Majesty's pleasure? It is such anomalies as this that contain the very germs of Socialism and Anarchy, which are all too easily propagated by paid professional agitators. (JW Dickenson)

⚜

A clearer case of insanity I have never met with or heard of. I have practised the profession of the law for thirty-one years, which is my justification for presuming to express an opinion on the matter. There is one point upon which I think some explanation is due.

---

28 In 1882, Lord Frederick Cavendish, Chief Secretary for Ireland and Thomas Henry Burke, Permanent Under-secretary were slain by members of 'Irish National Invincibles'. Seven men were involved; five were executed and two, accessories, were sentenced to long prison terms.

Why has not the counsel in the case come forward to state why a plea of insanity was not set up at the trial? The subject was referred to in your paper. So far as I am aware, the counsel in this case has preserved complete silence on the point. An explanation should be forthcoming on this point, and the Home Secretary induced even at the last moment to grant a reprieve. If the lawyers in the case knew nothing of the poor woman's antecedents, her family history, and of the witnesses who were prepared to depose from their personal knowledge to her condition of mental degeneracy, then all the more reason would there be for Sir Matthew Ridley not to act on the mere opinion of Drs Nicolson and Brayn. (HVC)

⚜

The Reverend GW Pope, Baptist minister of Shepherd's Bush, for four years a member of the Metropolitan Asylums Board, was particularly upset. Very late, just before midnight on July 16th, he called at the offices of the *Daily Chronicle* which had been supporting the *Daily Mail* crusade. Knowledgeable about mental matters, he was a good man, and he was very tired, but he wanted to find out if there was anything else that could be done. Although the Board and Leavesden Asylum had so far been immune from censure, Mr Pope, an insider, broke ranks, and indicated that the Board had a special responsibility. 'It appears,' the *Daily Chronicle* commented, 'that the murdered girl ate her cake on a Friday night, but that, although she was taken ill almost immediately, her condition was not brought to the attention of any of the medical men attached to the asylum until the following Tuesday – the day on which she died.

'Mr Pope, with Dr Prescott, formed the committee which was due to visit the asylum at the time of Ansell's death. When the day came, Dr Prescott was otherwise engaged, and Mr Pope alone investigated the case. Hence his interest in it. He contends that had the girl received the attention which she ought to have had her life might have been saved, and in these circumstances the least that the Board could have done was to join in the application to the Home Secretary. Mr Pope has been unable, however, to carry his colleagues with him.' In fact, he nearly did; at the second Ansell debate held on July 15th, there was, on a vote, a tight majority decision amid ill-feeling and loud uproar unprecedented at the Board meetings, which were open to the press, that an appeal would not be made to the Home Secretary. Such an appeal would have been weighty, as coming from the Asylums Board itself, knowing that there was undoubtedly imbecility in the family. 'It might not be insanity,' Mr Pope said knowledgeably now, 'but no one can know, as I do, the wretchedly poor stock from which the convict comes without realising that she must be an imbecile, if ever there was one.' The *Daily Chronicle* made the point that, 'Terrible as is the crime, and horrible the death of the murdered sister, it was probably stimulated by a desire to imitate other crimes of the same kind reported in the papers, which spread infection to this miserable, ignorant, half-witted person.'

Mr RD Yelverton, ex Chief Justice of the Bahamas, who had presided over many capital trials overseas, and was now practising at the London Bar, was fast becoming unpopular with the Home Office, and his epistolary style was sounding like Dr Forbes Winslow's at his sonorous peak. 'The girl's defence should have been based both on requiring proof of the deed by her and on evidence showing hereditary tendency to imbecility. These defences could easily have been welded together,' he argued annoyingly. With his exotic judicial background, he felt no obligation to hold back, was not at all inhibited, and fabulously outspoken. 'That she suffers from hereditary imbecility is at least a very strong presumption,' he continued. 'Justice requires, therefore, a careful inquiry by doctors, one of whom it is fair should represent her relatives: otherwise we are falling into the same error we condemn in the Dreyfus case.[29] I am confident that the full importance of various matters has not been thoroughly appreciated. I appeal through you (the *Daily Chronicle*) to the Home Secretary for a further consideration.'

---

29 The comparison with Dreyfus seems over-the-top. Ansell, although in the public eye, was scarcely an affair of state, and did not endanger the government, but this French miscarriage of justice, with its strong element of anti-semitism and its political complexities was still an issue in full spate in 1899. The secret court martial of Captain Alfred Dreyfus for passing documents to the German army was based on fabricated evidence - that was the 'error' - and Mr Yelverton was convinced that Mary Ann's guilt had not been properly proved.

The jury foreman, Charles Cusworth, was badly haunted by the case, and later said that he had done no work since the trial. On the morning of the 17th, he called at the *Daily Mail* and made a 'solemn statement' set out as a kind of informal affidavit. It caused great unease. He had aired his views, his repudiation of the verdict, previously but now that the sentence was firm, his words had more impact. He said:

> I am very deeply upset at seeing the decision of the Home Secretary to hang Mary Ansell. If her counsel had urged the plea of insanity, and had put before us the evidence which has since been published, which I have followed very closely, we should have been unanimous, I am sure, in recommending a commutation of the death sentence.
>
> No hint, to the best of my belief of insanity was, however, brought forward in the case; and in view of the facts laid before us at the trial we could not bring in anything but the severe naked verdict we did.
>
> With our experience of other cases we had it in our minds that, although we were bringing in a verdict of guilty, we had no idea that she would really be hanged. The common remark, in the jury's deliberations, was, "She won't be hanged, of course, but we must bring her in guilty on the evidence."
>
> If that one plea of insanity had been brought forward and put in evidence, as you have made it clear it might have been, we should certainly have recommended her strongly to mercy.
>
> I believe that the lack of mercy shown in this case will have such an effect on juries that they will in future be reluctant to bring in a verdict of condemnation in similar cases.

Lest this statement should be thought the over-sensitive reaction of one individual to the criminal courts – and he was, anyway, selected by his fellows as a wise and objective leader – another member of the dismayed jury, Mr HJ Wise, of Lee Cottage, Drayton Road, Elstree, Herts, wrote independently to the *Daily Mail*:

> As a result of the facts concerning her reason which have come to light since the trial, I fully expected that Ansell would be reprieved. So confidently I expected her sentence would be modified that I thought no word of mine could make the slightest difference. In your issue of this morning I read that the girl is to be hanged! Where a man's or a woman's life is concerned, proprieties should not be considered. As the counsel for the defence (I could not wish for a more able defender in any case) did not raise the point, and no evidence was produced

to show the state of the accused's mind, we felt that as "business" men we could not add a rider [for mercy] to the verdict of guilty. But had the facts which have since appeared concerning Mary Ann Ansell's state of mind and her family's history been presented to us, our verdict would have been such that the girl could not have been (as it seems she will be) hanged.

Unfortunately, what never appears is the reason why the jury, even without the later revelations, had thought Mary Ann insane enough for a rider of mercy, if only they had thought it proper to articulate their instinct, against the attitude of the judge. Was it the girl's facial features and 'sullen' demeanour, the outrageous crime itself, or was it a flow of rumour, a current, during the proceedings, that made them suspicious about her mental state?

Published afterthoughts by the jury were unsettling enough for the Home Office, where the officials were clinging on to the secret advice of the Broadmoor doctors, but treachery by the treasured expert handwriting witness, Thomas Henry Gurrin, could have provided more embarrassment, except that as a paid expert witness for the Crown, he felt obliged to write directly to the Home Secretary, where his letter was filed away and remained as secret as the medical reports. His comments are probably not so important as those of the jury, but they have a corroborative value.

'Sir,' [Mr Gurrin wrote on July 17th], 'I was one of the witnesses for the Crown in the prosecution of this wretched girl, and was compelled to give very damning evidence against her in connection with her handwriting. I have seen her from the first during the proceedings at Watford as well as at the Trial and as I felt sure that those most competent to judge of her mental capacity would advise against the extreme penalty of the law in this case I have abstained from either signing the petition for mercy or from making any communication to the public press.

Now however that I see it announced publicly that the law is to take its course, I feel bound to ask you to pardon me for bringing to your notice two facts which came under my immediate observation, and which probably have not been brought to your notice:-

The first was an instance which occurred during the proceedings before the magistrates at Watford. The counsel for the accused while cross-examining one of the witnesses in reference to the sale of the poison made some allusion to Keating's powder in some jocular way. My eyes were at the moment on the face of the accused who was crying up to that moment, but on catching the humorous allusion to the flea powder her face suddenly broke out into smiles, fully appreciating and apparently quite enjoying the humour. This instance of levity under such terrible circumstances seemed to me to be incompatible with a sane mind capable of recognising the gravity of the proceedings and their issue.

The second fact was this. I travelled up to town immediately after the trial in the company of several of the jurors who had tried the case, and heard them state they would be much relieved if they felt that the law would not be carried out, as they could scarcely believe that she was fully responsible. Yet it did not occur to them at the time to add any recommendation to mercy. [A prime specimen of hearsay for Charles Murdoch, and not helpful to Mary Ann if it merely 'did not occur' to the jury to add the rider.] I make no appeal to you. I desire simply to be permitted to lay before you these two facts that are within my knowledge, feeling that if they are of any value, I shall not be able to reproach myself for having remained silent.

Mr Yelverton was on terms with Dr Forbes Winslow over the Ansell cause, and on July 18th, he sent a letter to 'Sir Matthew'. Typewritten, from the Temple, it contained a threat, and its tone was found objectionable:

I intend to be present at the hurriedly summoned Cannon Street Hotel Meeting today, and am handing over a brief at the Law Courts to be able to attend.

I think if Mary Ansell is executed, it will be an iniquity, and so horrible is it that a friendless girl should be simply done to death, that I respectfully state I shall, if she is executed, fulfil a duty upon me as a tolerably wealthy and independent member of the Bar, to analyse in the form of a publication the circumstances attending and following her conviction. I shall collate the facts which have appeared in *The Times*, *Daily Mail*, and other papers, carefully analyse the circumstances, and compare your previous exercises of the Royal prerogative, and shall not spare pains in having such circumstances widely known.

I would respectfully say here, how can you ignore the strong representations made, including the debate on the Asylums Board, and the statements to you of jurymen?

As to the report of the Superintendent of Broadmoor, it is open from his official position and for other reasons, to very serious objection.

His taking part in the inquiry invalidates it, as for one thing he is not an independent doctor; there are also other objections to him.

I feel so strongly for the friendless position of this unfortunate girl, that I shall devote a considerable portion of my time, if she is hung, to impressing upon the country the utter insecurity which exists for justice being done, or even the reasons for justice being inquired into, a short respite being all that we seek, to be accompanied by an independent inquiry.'

Charles Murdoch thought, of course, that Yelverton was letting the side down: 'An extraordinary letter for a QC, and an Ex Colonial judge. It has appeared in the press already.' From a later perspective, the hints about Dr Brayn are interesting. What were the 'other objections'?' We may note, too, that Mr Yelverton is careful not to impute professional incompetence to the defence lawyers in the Ansell case.

A late letter, headed hopefully, 'Fresh Evidence', from the Ansells' landlord, Joseph Bangs, of 142 High Street, Camden Town, was published in the *Daily Mail*:

Am grieved to hear that the Home Secretary has refused to mitigate the sentence passed upon that unfortunate and misguided girl, Mary Ansell. As the owner of the house which has been occupied by her family for many years, they have particularly come under my notice, and have always considered them generally possessed of very weak intellects, some more than others. From my knowledge of Mary Ansell, I certainly do not consider her capable of judging her own actions or being responsible for them. Should this poor girl suffer the death sentence, I consider it would be a disgrace to our country.

Mrs Ayres, the Manchester Street School teacher, called at the *Daily Mail* offices, with her husband, to reiterate her previous strong statement, and offered to make a solemn affidavit if the Home Secretary would receive it.

Percy Wisbey had given up all hope. The *Daily Chronicle* sent a journalist to see him on the night of the 17th. He was in sombre mood:

I am afraid that I can add nothing to the sum total of your information, nor suggest any further steps that can be taken. Every endeavour possible has been made to save this unfortunate woman's life, but I have received a letter from the Home Secretary couched in similar terms to that which was sent to Mr Jobson. As soon as the trial was concluded, petitions were prepared. One was circulated in Hemel Hempstead by Mr W Bird, and was signed by the vicar and about 150 others: my own petition was sent to London to the office of the *Daily Mail*, where about 500 names were attached; and there was a third got up by Mr Jobson.

As to why the question of the prisoner's sanity was not raised at the time of the trial, I can only say that there were many difficulties in the way, and it was only after careful consideration that we took the course we did. Had the plea of insanity been put forward then the prosecution could have produced expert evidence on the point, and if we had been unable to controvert it the jury would have convicted her straight away, and we should have had no subsequent loophole for appeal. That is why we acted as we did.

This is very lame, a dire confession of lack of confidence. No insane person would have wanted to be represented by this pair of lawyers. By his argument, the plea of insanity was too risky even to be put, which is ridiculous. Nobly, perhaps, he does not fall back upon his lack of funding. He fails always to address his failure to gather the strong evidence of 'imbecility', and he does not face up to the fact that a *late* plea of insanity was very likely to fail in our judicial system at the time. Mary Ann would have cut a perfectly convincing figure silent in the dock, sullen or crying as her peculiarities were described by a string of responsible witnesses. She did not need to be gibbering or lunging. In fact, the weak defence, which was scarcely worth pursuing, however eloquently counsel argued the medical issues in some fantasy of greatness, was dicing with the client's life. If a stronger defence had been available, if, say, there had been no handwriting evidence, the perceived risk might have been reduced. And of course there was then no 'appeal', only a fragile 'plea for mercy'.

To stand fairly, however, against these adverse comments, but not to eliminate them, the vexed case of Charles Maidment, the 'Swanwick Tragedy', should be brought into the debate. Here there was a capital trial which took place on June 27th, 1899, a couple of days before *Ansell*, (June 29th to 30th), but at a different Assize, the

Hampshire Court at Winchester, under Mr Justice Wright.[30] It could have concentrated the mind of William Clarke Hall at the last minute, being a perfect example of the failure of the insanity plea, although brought in due form, prepared to the hilt, and put to the jury with a full complement of evidence. Execution was the outcome. It was not a matter of the prisoner's being unfit to plead, but of showing that he was insane at the time of the commission of the murder.

This was a rustic affair, coming from unrequited love. Charles Maidment, aged twenty-two, was an agricultural labourer, but not of the poorest background. He worked for his great uncle at his fruit orchard in Swanwick, a small village. Two miles away lived with her father, a market gardener, at Pavilion Villa, Dorcas Houghton, aged eighteen. For one year, Charles and Dorcas had been sweethearts, seen wandering romantically along the flowered lanes. There was an understanding, although not a formal engagement. Possibly she had some doubts about him, and it was known that he had never been to her home.

For an equal length of time, a twelvemonth, he had proudly owned a large, heavy revolver, and always had it with him. He was thought to be clumsy: he shot himself in the finger and needed medical treatment. On April 18th, 1899, Dorcas told Charles that she wanted to break off their relationship and would like to meet him the following evening at 6 pm, so that she could return the little

30 Sir Robert Samuel Wright, (1839–1904) Balliol, Inner Temple, 1861, Judge of the Queen's Bench Division, 1891. When sentencing Maidment to death, he made no observation of his own. One of the worried members of the public, 'A Hampshire Clergyman', had some good observations to make, writing to the Editor of the *Daily Mail* (July 10th). 'On Tuesday, June 10th, business as a waiting witness compelled me to hear a portion of the trial — the condemnation and death sentence of a young man for murdering his sweetheart at Swanwick, near Botley. I sat close to the dock. He gave me the impression of being a dull, heavy, melancholic being. His counsel urged as strong facts in favour of his insanity as any I have read in connection with the condemned woman Ansell. But Mr Justice Wright told the jury that any question of the prisoner's sanity would be inquired into by experts (at the order of the Home Secretary, I presume). In passing sentence, the judge simply repeated the words of the sentence, and added not a single word. Yet I have seen no letter, no signs of agitation on his behalf. Is mercy only for criminals in or near London? In both cases let us trust to the wisdom of the Home Secretary who is no bloodthirsty man willing to sign the death warrant of any unfortunate sentenced to death.'

presents which he had given to her. He was heartbroken and got up unusually early the next morning. He soon abandoned his work and set off to the village. His uncle met him on his way back and asked where he had been. 'Only up Spettisbury', [his home] he said. The old man told how, 'He looked very strange at me. His eyes pierced at me, and I was rather frightened.' Henry Fielder, the postman, saw him next, walking in Swanwick Lane with Dorcas, who was carrying a small brown paper parcel. Returning from his round, he saw in a final tableau, the girl sitting reading on the grass, and Charles leaning on a gate. Then a single shot was heard, and Charles was glimpsed, 'tearing about the fields in a wild manner.' The body of the girl was found at the verge of the lane with a death wound behind her left ear, the face burnt and scorched. One large bullet had been fired from a distance of twelve inches and was lodged in the brain. Charles made his way to Fareham police station, gave himself up, and confessed.

Maidment did not give evidence on his own behalf. Mr Clavell Salter defended him extremely well: his client's one joy in life had been taken from him, and it was too much for an already weak brain. The mental balance was upset. The uncle attested to his nephew's previous oddness; at times he was silent for long periods and at others acted more like a child. His temper was queer, and he (the uncle) had told him that he was not in his right mind, and was 'ruled by the moon'. Dr Cade, who had attended him in 1898 for his injured finger, considered him to be a morose person: melancholia was frequently betrayed by moroseness. However, Dr TD Richards, the prison medical officer, with eleven years' experience in that rôle, considered him somewhat depressed, but with no 'aberration' whatsoever. He knew nothing of any family history. Cross-examined, he did concede that Maidment was a man of low intellect.

Counsel proceeded to bring witnesses as to the maternal heredity of mental disease; the prisoner's mother's parents, he stated, had the taint of insanity for three generations. (In this case, lunatic asylums were going to be identified, and there would be slight opportunity for official complaints of 'hearsay'.) Thomas Cuff,

Maidment's grandfather, was brought to say that his wife's cousin was in the Dorset County Lunatic Asylum, after attacking his wife with a hammer. Another cousin, Samuel Hopkins, died in Fisherton Asylum, and his son, also Samuel, was in Charminster Asylum. The witness's niece, Mary Cuff, was in an unnamed asylum. The witness's daughter, Harriett Sibley, had had frequent epileptic fits.

The grandfather was moved on to evidence as to the boy's previous signs of insanity. Charles had lived with him from the age of two. He was an orphan, with two brothers. He would go for two or three days without saying a word, and then be quite lively. He used to hallo and scream at night, say he was going a-fishing, and try to climb out of the window. Sometimes he sat in a corner, crying, and sweating big drops of perspiration. Once he nearly drowned, having jumped or fallen into the water. Afterwards, he suffered from a discharge of the nose and ears, was always complaining about his head, and seemed 'rum'.

The obviously experienced defence had taken the trouble to call in a doctor to examine Maidment in prison before the trial. Dr Brown testified that he had thirty years' experience, and was medical officer to the Winchester Union (ie Workhouse). In his experience, the prisoner's mind was neither healthy nor normal. He had a homicidal tendency of impulsive character. The maternal taint came from both sides of the mother's family and would therefore affect the mind. The alternate fits of depression and excitement indicated a diseased mind.

Res ipsa loquitur, one would have thought, but a disapproving judge was seated aloft. Mr Clavell Salter, arguing for insanity 'drawn in with his mother's milk', made the point, so crucial at that time, that premeditation was not proved. The Crown insisted that the murder was an act of vengeance, and that the evidence of insanity was doubtful.

How would the Judge react to the defence? Was he going to be like Judge Mathew? Of course he was! 'The fact that a person's grandmother's cousin was lunatic did not necessarily prove his insanity,' Judge Wright summed up. He himself, he said, would not put much weight on that evidence. (He gave no consideration to the signs of earlier insanity.) The claim, he said, that the prisoner was insane when he fired the shot 'was a sort of defence that was not likely to be believed in.' After such an address, the jury delivered a verdict of Guilty, in ten minutes, and the judge told them that that was absolutely the right verdict.

All the hard work of the defence lay in ruins: only the plea for mercy was left. It is interesting that the judge did not insert the coded message (see Chapter Five) that he would be opposed to mercy. In another difference from the Ansell case, the judge expressly advised the jury that, even if they found the prisoner guilty, the Secretary of State would have power to call in the best medical evidence to decide the man's mental condition. When sentencing Maidment to death, he made no observation of his own. Maidment had something to say – he did not know what he was doing when he did it. Two medical officers were indeed appointed by Sir Matthew White Ridley, and found against insanity. Their names were Dr Nicolson and Dr Brayn.

Dr Forbes Winslow, simmering, had worked himself into a froth of genuine frustration and indignation. He made a last attempt to influence the Home Secretary on a personal level by despatching, on July 18th, a typewritten letter which was unfortunately marred by blocks of capitals, producing a deranged impression.

> Sir, Having been fully instructed in this Case by Mr Wisbey Solicitor for the defence I feel it my duty to draw your attention to two matters. 1st The statement of The Rev. Henry Fowler, the Chaplain of St Albans Gaol which is as follows "I REALLY CANNOT SAY THAT THE UNFORTUNATE GIRL COMPREHENDS THE GUILT OF THE CRIME OF WHICH SHE HAS BEEN CONVICTED. I HAVE VISITED HER DAILY AND HAVE TALKED AND READ TO HER IN THE MINISTRATION OF RELIGIOUS COMFORT, BUT IT IS VERY DIFFICULT TO SAY, AND I REALLY CANNOT SAY, THAT SHE UNDERSTANDS THE GRAVITY OF THE OFFENCE". The statement here made in every way coincided with my previous report furnished at the request of the Solicitor to you.
>
> Commenting on this, Mr Charles Cusworth, of Warwick House, Capel Road, New Bushey Foreman of the Jury, states "IF HER COUNSEL HAD URGED THE PLEA OF INSANITY AND HAD PUT BEFORE US THE EVIDENCE WHICH HAS SINCE BEEN PUBLISHED WHICH I HAVE

FOLLOWED VERY CLOSELY WE SHOULD HAVE BEEN UNANIMOUS, I AM SURE IN RECOMMENDING A COMMUTATION OF THE DEATH SENTENCE".

The rule of law laid down in the McNaughton case, and subsequently confirmed by the Judges in the House of Law Lords in 1843 and which is still in existence at the present day is as follows "That to establish a defence on the grounds of Insanity it must be clearly proved that at the time of the act that the accused was labouring under such a defect of reason from a diseased mind, as not to know the nature and quality of the act he was doing, or if he did know, that he did not know that he was doing wrong."

I respectfully maintain on the Prisoner's behalf, tho not having been permitted to examine her, that by the statement made by Mr Fowler the wretched girl did not understand the difference between right and wrong and is therefore not a responsible person.

I would again respectfully suggest, and this action on my part is not mere agitation, but based upon a large experience, as you doubtless are aware of Criminal Lunacy, and with the sole desire to save this person's life, that you advise her Majesty to graciously give a further respite of one week, to enable you to verify the correctness or otherwise of the views expressed by the Chaplain of the prison.

To me it does not appear to be a question for expert evidence, but one of common sense, which any reasonable person could decide, the issue is DOES MARY ANSELL, NOW STANDING AS A CONVICTED CRIMINAL, UNDERSTAND HER POSITION? IS SHE CONSCIOUS OF THE GRAVITY OF THE ACT COMMITTED BY HER? CAN SHE DISCRIMINATE BETWEEN RIGHT AND WRONG? The Chaplain evidently, who has seen her daily and frequently, says no, if so I claim on behalf of the girl, mercy and justice and would ask for a respite of one week to verify these statements.

This doomed document, with its air of desperation, is far from Dr Forbes Winslow's best work. Driven to invoke commonsense in his search for a point of entry into the official carapace, he is deserting all the ideals of his proud expertise. It may be that he judges Sir Matthew to be unsympathetic to mental niceties, impatient of *McNaughton*, and more open to appeal as a reasonable man. The Home Office was riled: it was a tense time, with a whiff of rebellion, and Charles Murdoch wrote a longer minute than he usually thought appropriate: 'The Chaplain has done a great deal of mischief unfortunately by his misguided statements. Far from not realising the position it was apparent from the statement made by the Examining Doctors that the prisoner intended to reserve any statement to the prison officials to the last and was apparently most calculating in her behaviour. The points submitted by Dr Winslow were all cleared up by the report of the Examining Doctors – namely that she fully recognised her position, knew what she was doing, and did it for a purpose.'

These remarks are puzzling. There may be a distinction here between the Broadmoor doctors' official report and some 'statement', possibly oral, made by those doctors. There is certainly nothing in the actual report about reserving a statement to the last, and no opinion expressed there about the prisoner's being 'most calculating' which is only an unsubstantiated opinion, anyway.

Stubbornly arguing on, Dr Forbes Winslow made his last appeal in the only forum available open to him – the *Daily Mail* of July 18th. He enlarged on the comparison with Richard Prince,[31] who, he said, 'committed a well-planned, premeditated murder with malice prepense and the jury found that "he was conscious of the gravity of his act and its consequences". But because he had been held eccentric, he was held not answerable for his actions, and was acquitted on the ground of insanity, and this in the face of the rule of law laid down'. Mary Ann Ansell, the doctor said, was ignorant of the difference between right and wrong, and unaware of the gravity of her act. Referring to the chaplain's remarks, he went on to say that, 'If there ever was a poor, weak-minded fool, here is one, if we are to believe – and *I see no reason in any way to discredit it* (author's italics) – the history of the case and the affidavits made by her former employers... *Possibly there may be nothing objective in her condition, no outward sign of anything indicative of insanity*, so often seen in criminals who are assuming it. No, there is only observable in her that stolid behaviour, disregard and complete indifference for what she has done, or what is about to be done to her ... so often seen in those mentally afflicted, whose brains are improperly developed, and in cases of mental degeneration when the disease, as

---

31 v. Chapter Seven, fn 19.

in this case, is inherited.' He argues that precedent might have been set aside and Mary Ann Ansell's own advisors allowed to examine her in addition to the government doctors. 'I feel very strongly on this point, and the old adage, "*Audi alteram partem*", is a good one.. I hardly think that "red tapeism" should stand in the way.'

Tuesday, July 18th, was the last day of hope, and frenzied activity was going on, as the Government held firm.[32] Dr Forbes Winslow's name was heard in the House of Commons: if he could have risen to his feet there himself on that occasion, he would have done so. Generally, he was avowedly not at all interested in politics. James Henry Dalziel (1868-1935) Liberal, knighted in 1908, a young radical with a background in journalism, was there to ask questions in a last-ditch atmosphere. On the previous day, he had asked if the Home Secretary had considered the insanity in the Ansell family, and the fact that Dr Forbes Winslow, the eminent specialist had pronounced as his emphatic opinion that the prisoner was not responsible for her action; and, further, that no evidence on the question of insanity was produced at the trial; and whether he had any objection to the publication of the report of the two experts appointed to inquire into the case.

Sight of the report would not, actually have favoured the prisoner, because many of her supporters would have been shocked by her admissions. However, some form of early 'data protection' of the

32 A late rumour about Broadmoor, seen as a mysterious removed place (actually disapproved of by Dr Forbes Winslow, see *The Insanity of Passion and Crime*, p. 241) sprang up and was allowed space in the *Daily Mail*, under the heading of Broadmoor Too Full: "It is well-known to people in the East-hampstead district that Broadmoor is full to overflowing with lunatics, and additional buildings have been sanctioned to accommodate the new arrivals. Numbers are in Broadmoor at the present time who are not insane. Persons who have committed the most horrible murders are today using edge tools in the several working parties, with attendants looking after them, who are not armed with even a stick to defend them. Prince, the murderer of poor Terriss, is one of the sanest men in Broadmoor, and there are several related to wealthy people, who are no more insane than the attendants themselves. Persons are continually being sent to Broadmoor, writes a correspondent, who ought to have had the rope round their necks for the vile crimes they have committed. As many men as possible are being sent to their county asylums, because there is no room for them at Broadmoor. Why should the officials therefore, be burdened with additional people when they have a chance to stop it? I do not say they have thought of this in Mary Ansell's case. But this inference may be drawn."

individual was not the rationale for the refusal to disclose. It was rather the precedent of holding back such reports that was being jealously guarded. Dalziel expected the stonewalling reply, but he had put the formal question on record. The Home Secretary intoned: 'Following the course which has always been adopted by my predecessors, I must decline to lay before the House a report made for the purpose of assisting me in giving advice to Her Majesty, for which I alone am responsible. (Cheers) I may, however, state that all the circumstances of the case, including the family history of the convict, were most anxiously considered by me, as well as by all those who assisted me. The opinion of Dr Forbes Winslow, who was, however, not consulted by me, was also before me, and was fully considered.'

Then, on the Tuesday, Dalziel returned to the attack, asking the Home Secretary if he was aware of the statement made by the foreman of the jury. Sir Matthew White Ridley: 'My attention has been drawn to a statement which has appeared in the newspapers. [There had been no direct approach from Mr Cusworth.] *I am satisfied as the result of a very full enquiry and after consultation with the Judge, that if the question of insanity had been raised at the trial there is no evidence to that effect which could properly have affected the verdict of the jury.*' (Author's italics.) This is an astounding representation, but there was no one there to refute it, and it was the wrong forum. There *could have been* evidence as to insanity which could properly have affected the verdict of the jury.

'I fear,' the Home Secretary continued with this uncomfortable exchange, 'the answer to the last paragraph [Dalziel's request for a postponement of execution pending an independent inquiry into the prisoner's sanity] must be in the negative.' He gave no reason. 'It is my duty,' he added 'to protest against the insinuation which appears to be conveyed by the word, "independent".'

Dalziel climbed down, and looked to his own reputation in Parliament: 'As a personal explanation, I wish to be allowed to explain that the word, "independent" means officers not retained by the Home Office.' Finally, he asked about the prison chaplain's opinions.

Home Secretary: 'Every single point which has been alluded to by the honourable member has been fully within my knowledge during the last week, and I have given each of them my best attention.'[33]

A back-up note by Charles Murdoch on the growing demand for an independent inquiry 'justifies' the negative decision: 'The enquiry as to the prisoner's condition already held was the usual one – as prescribed by Statute in such cases namely that whenever in the case of a prisoner under sentence of death it appears to Secretary of State by any means that there is reason to believe that such a prisoner may be insane he is empowered to appoint two legally qualified medical officers to examine such prisoner and enquire as to his or her insanity and to report thereon to him. This course has been followed by himself and by his predecessors in office in all such cases, and the medical practitioners are those upon whose advice the Home Office has for many years past been accustomed to rely.'

---

33 HC Deb 18 July 1899 vol 74 cc1171-2.

CHAPTER TEN

STORMING THE HOUSE

> She comes of a family deeply tainted with insanity, and she has
> been nurtured in a corner of the unweeded city garden, where the
> doctrine of the sanctity of human life goes pretty much by default.
> We need not be greatly astonished that the face of murder looks out
> sometimes from quarters where a family life is impossible, where
> the new-born child is often a signal for the family's eviction, and the
> visits of the insurance collector are a perpetual reminder that death
> may be more profitable as well as more blessed than life.

In these terms, on July 18th, the *Daily Chronicle*, elegiac, sought to
rationalise the coming event.

In a different mood, the *Pall Mall Gazette*, a Conservative paper at
that time, so different from its jaunty coverage of Jack the Ripper,
showed no mercy:

> The poisoning was ...one of the most deliberately contrived
> murders that are recorded in the annals of crime. The sending of the
> phosphorus through the post and the forging of the letter from her
> mother [father] protesting against the post-mortem examination,
> stamp it as a masterpiece of perverted calculation. Admitted to give
> evidence on her own behalf, she adopted the extremely ingenious
> line that she had insured her sister's life to give her a nice funeral,
> thereby appealing to what is a strong motive with the poorer classes,
> and the poorer they are the stronger it is.

There was at this late stage a little, not much, personal criticism of
the Home Secretary:

> Sir Matthew White Ridley has not been entirely fortunate during
> his term of office, and in cases which have been left to his unaided
> but unobstructed judgment he has not satisfied the public mind. It

was he who commuted the death penalty in the case of Whitmarsh, and in that of Collins, and no man to this day knows, or ever will know, why, in two instances which were as nearly as possible equal, the punishment inflicted on the one should have been exactly twice as heavy as that imposed upon another.

A cross Charles Murdoch underlined the reference to Collins, and wrote in a side comment, 'No! How ignorantly people do write!' Nonetheless, the *Morning Herald*, here, was not opposing the execution, and was supportive of Drs Nicolson and Brayn:

> men of enormous experience, and it would be nothing short of madness to suppose that either of them could possibly nurture any kind of animus against the miserable woman whom they have examined....They were pledged to an unflinching presentation of the truth, and there is no imaginable reason to suppose that they have acted lightly, or without a full sense of responsibility, or without complete qualification. The Home Secretary had no option but to accept the judgment he had invited, and it is as unjust to assail him in respect to this matter as it is to assail the experts....There is quite unreasonable outcry in some quarters because Dr Forbes Winslow's opinion was not taken into account. Dr Forbes Winslow is a man of high attainment and wide experience, but he has not had the needful opportunity of personal access to the prisoner. Two gentlemen of equal attainment and experience have that advantage over him, and they have pronounced their judgment....

The *Daily Mail* was still fighting, while pointing out that neither the *Mail*, nor the *Daily Chronicle* had ever spoken a single ill word of the judge or the Home Secretary. The journal did argue that, 'the short reprieve which is usual to grant in order that further inquiry may be held should at least be given.'

On the afternoon of this last day, the Ansell protestors moved out into the open from their homes and offices and made their way to the meeting called by Mr Jobson at the great hall of the Cannon Street Hotel, where 'monster Meetings', as they were called, quaintly, had been held regarding the Staunton case (1877)[34] and the Maybrick

---

34 The famous 'Penge Mystery', actually not an insanity matter, after which Dr Forbes Winslow became, as he said, an agitator. The victim was 'weak-minded' and the four sentenced to death by Mr Justice Hawkins for her murder by starvation were very lucky to escape the gallows. The doctor helped to organise one of those 'giant meetings',

agitation of 1889. Dr Forbes Winslow relates that he had been summoned to act as chairman, but was incensed to find that this time the proprietor had banned the assembly on learning that the subject was the Ansell execution.

Several hundred people began to disperse, but many remained in the station yard outside the hotel, and an impromptu meeting was held *in situ*. It was a summer's day. Mr Yelverton of the Bahamas was there, naturally, and he, not Dr Forbes Winslow, was elected, with cheers, as chairman. He addressed the eager and vociferous crowd: it was not a fair trial; there was sufficient evidence for a postponement; the case exemplified one law for the rich, and another for the poor. (Shouts of "shame") A telegram was despatched forthwith to the Queen, praying for a stay of execution, and afterwards Mr Yelverton moved that a second revision of the Home Secretary's decision was called for on the grounds of new facts since conviction; Mary Ann Ansell's youth; the difference of medical opinion; *the defence being only half prepared and weakly put before the jury* (author's italics); the statement of the foreman and another juror as to their withholding a plea for mercy; and, 'That the case is one pre-eminently demanding a Court of Criminal Appeal where human life is at stake.'

A deputation of seven was chosen to storm the House of Commons and beard the Home Secretary. Messrs Yelverton, Jobson, Cusworth and the Reverend GW Pope of the Asylums Board, putting in a brave appearance, together with three members of Parliament, backed up by some of the crowd, then marched off to Pump Court, Temple, at Mr Yelverton's invitation, for another open-air meeting. A demand was made for the publication of the Nicolson/Brayn report. Onwards, then, to the Home Office, Dr Forbes Winslow with them, he says, where they were met by an official, who told them that the Home Secretary was not in, but if a communication were to be left, it would be handed to him. 'Exciting scenes' took place in the lobby of the House, where a large body of people, headed by a determined Charles Cusworth pushed in and succeeded in obtaining over 100

where he stated publicly that all the post-mortem indications pointed to brain disease caused by tuberculosis. All four were reprieved.

signatures of members to an impromptu, handwritten petition. The Home Office preserved the columns of names. The main petition prayed for a postponement of execution for at least a week for further inquiry, 'seeing that a great diversity of opinion exists thereon', and a supplementary petition asking for postponement for a short time was, apparently, signed by members who arrived later. Discomforted and frustrated, the protestors dispersed.

According to Dr Forbes Winslow, the petition 'was signed by one hundred Liberal members, but I regret to say that it became a political question, whilst the Conservative members, for some reason best known to themselves, supported their Home Secretary.' A little study of the names shows this absolute division to be not strictly true. The petition was handed to Sir Matthew late in the evening. At 6 o'clock, Mr Jobson had sent a telegram to Sir Arthur Bigge, the Queen's private secretary, at Windsor, to ask if it would be possible for the Sovereign to receive representations with a view to a respite on the ground that further evidence of insanity had been obtained. The common people, and some more sophisticated, still held to a touching faith in the ability of the mother Queen, in her own right, to save a convict from the scaffold. Sadly, they were misguided: it was an illusion. By Section I of the Criminal Statutes Repeal Act 1861, the judges lost their right of reprieve, which they had held since 1837, and the Home Secretary alone was entitled to exercise that legal power.

The Queen retained her Royal Prerogative of Mercy, but she was to exercise it *only on the 'advice' of the Home Secretary*.[35] There was no official submission to the Queen from the Home Office, and the papers were not even sent to her. Although she could not 'interfere' with a death sentence, she could and did discuss certain cases with her Home Secretary, and her views could have an occult influence. When Sir William Harcourt (a Liberal) held the office, he did have some unfortunate brushes with his Queen about the Prerogative.

---

35 The entire history and effect of the power of reprieve possessed by the Home Secretaries is to be found in *Reprieve: A Study of a System* (1965) by the late Fenton Bresler, writer and barrister, greatly missed.

She thought that he was too lenient, especially to men who killed their wives. He set out in a letter to her the three main principles which guided him in his advice to her: compassion: a possibility of an unjust conviction; the precept that mercy should be shown where there was no intention to kill. Harcourt's influence pervaded the Home Office until the effective end of hanging in 1957.

The Queen was kept at a distance from the Ansell case. Aged 80, she was *compos mentis* but failing in her bodily constitution. In May, 1899, she had returned from a holiday in the south of France. She was not likely to have felt compassion for Mary Ann, due to her strong feelings for the sanctity of the family. Notoriously, she had not wanted Florence Maybrick to be spared, after being convicted of the murder of her husband, and here there was sororicide. She would not have been moved by the girl's plight, even though she was, as a matter of fact, sympathetic to the sufferings of the poor, had studied the matter, especially when young, and wished for reform. As for her attitude to 'idiots and imbeciles', she had been enlightened and interested. In 1862, she had conferred a Royal Charter on Earlswood Asylum, having subscribed 250 guineas in the name of Edward Prince of Wales, who had laid the foundation stone in 1853. Queen Victoria cannot be blamed for having a less philanthropic reaction to outright insanity, since deluded 'lunatics' were always shooting at her!

Now, on July 18th, 1899, Mr Jobson received by return a short reply: 'Queen cannot receive deputation. Your representation must be made through the Secretary of State. Bigge.' It is sad to read the many, preserved telegrams (some 66) which, all that long day, her Majesty's humble servants had been sending in good faith to Windsor Castle where Sir Arthur raked them in and presented them the next day to the Home Office where they were marked 'after the execution'. Lower and middle classes thought it worth a try, including several members of Parliament 'on behalf of Mr Dalziel'. Those pleading often referred to Mary Ann's 'imbecility', not her 'lunacy': the *Daily Mail*'s 'new evidence' had obviously had an effect. Early in the morning, Percy Wisbey's innocent message was, 'Will not your most Gracious Majesty intervene to save the life of Mary Ansell to be executed tomorrow.' Dr Forbes Winslow's approach is typical of his character: 'I am of opinion that Mary Ansell is not responsible I have had complete history and statements placed before me and I cannot entertain the slightest doubt as to her mental state my view is I believe fully endorsed by Prison Chaplain who has seen her daily...' More tentatively, Dr JM Winn, of 87 Goldhurst Terrace, NW, who was actually Dr Forbes Winslow's aged father-in-law, asked 'I hope Your Majesty will pardon my appeal on behalf of poor ignorant imbecile girl Mary Ansell to be executed tomorrow morning I am a retired Lunacy Physician and I [never] knew in my great experience of a case which so earnestly called for the exercise of Your Royal prerogative.'

Few lawyers sent a telegram: an exception reads tersely, 'Ansell support Foreman Jury's appeal Yelverton late Chief Justice Bahamas'. Cantley, of the Stock Exchange, said pithily, 'God save you You save her.' A crowded meeting of 'Citizens of London' held without objection at the Cannon Street Hotel asked for postponement. A typical appeal from the people would be, 'A loyal subject entreats Her Majesty to grant a reprieve to the poor imbecile Mary Ansell preserve thou her who is appointed to die will Her Majesty graciously take note of the prison Chaplain's opining may the Lord grant my earnest appeal to Her Majesty Copeland Skindles Maidenhead' and another prays, 'I crave your Most Gracious Majesty to exercise your Royal prerogative of Mercy and to pardon the helpless and unfortunately insane girl Mary Ansell 21 years of age her prostrated and aged parents together with thousands of your subjects will have additional reason for blessing their Queen. Nino Hassan 23 Warrington Crescent London.'

Sir Arthur Bigge received a telegram at 7.30 pm: 'Signatures of Probably approaching one hundred members will be presented to Home Secretary at ten o'clock tonight asking for short respite for Mary Ansell several Peers support pray do what you can City Deputation.' At 10 o'clock that night, Mr Jobson sent in a communication to the Home Secretary, who was still at the House of Commons, to inform him about the negative terms of the telegram from Sir Arthur Bigge.

Sir Matthew had always treated him with courtesy, and now he replied in an autograph letter: 'Sir, I have just received your note. I have no command from her Majesty, and I do not see how I can make an exception to the rule of not receiving deputations on criminal cases. I have given, with my advisers, every consideration to all the facts brought before me, and I regret to be obliged to adhere to the decision which I have given.'

⁕

Half-forgotten in the background, on that last Tuesday, the Ansell family had an appointment at St Albans. Somehow, they missed their train, and arrived late and agitated at the gates of the prison just after 3 o'clock. It was reported that Mary Ann had begun to think that they were not coming, and did not care about her fate. Her visitors made up a contingent of five – her parents, and, on a second permit, three of her cousins, one with a baby in arms. The cousins saw her first, then James and Sarah, for about only half-an-hour each. Mr Edward Lloyd, the chief warder and her two special wardresses were present throughout. The parents found their daughter very changed in appearance since their last visit. The small cell was well-lighted, and her care-worn features, bony and shadowed showed up in harsh relief.

The mother was racked with tears, and the father, although he tried to control his grief, was not much better. 'The poor girl seemed quite dead within herself, James told a journalist afterwards. 'She could not bring herself to believe that she had to die. She seemed quite worn-out, in a kind of stupor, and had little to say. She just leaned against the grating helplessly. I told her to live in hope if she died in despair, and she seemed to cheer up. She still thinks she won't be hanged and so do I. I shall keep hoping right down to the last moment.' It was strange, he said, that this would be his third child to die without the comfort of their mother and father. 'He thanked the public for taking up his daughter's case. It was very pleasing to him to find that a poor man should get such sympathy and support.

"Do you forgive me, father?" said she after a time. "Yes, certainly, my girl," said I. "If I don't forgive you, how can I expect to be forgiven myself? That seemed to comfort her. She didn't seem to have expected us to forgive her.' He had not asked her a lot of questions because he was afraid of upsetting her. Then the family were gone, travelling back home through the countryside. They left behind some sense of hope, and at the prison, too, someone must have been whispering to her that a reprieve was still possible.

The Reverend Henry Fowler had been a constant and consoling visitor, several times on the last day. He read to her from the Scriptures, which were familiar to her, calling on all his experience to comfort and reconcile. He was known to be deeply distressed. For Mary Ann, he was a personification of the authority figures who had tried to guide and improve her before she did something terrible. On the Monday, Miss Frost, her old Sunday School teacher, had been allowed to see her. It was made known that the condemned girl had been provided with a new dress and shoes for her final walk in this world. She could not go out in rags and tatters. 'Some ladies called at the prison and left flowers to be given to the doomed woman.'

Another visitor, unknown to Mary Ann, Billington, the executioner, entered the building quietly and took up his quarters, before preparing and honing his apparatus, with the assistance of a local carpenter. The chief warder had made the preliminary arrangements on the previous day; the scaffold had been brought over from Bedford. Billington had come straight from Winchester where he had just despatched Charles Maidment. One day separated the two unfortunates. Both of them went quietly. A report on the Maidment hanging stated that, 'The head was lying right over on the left shoulder, in a manner which indicated a broken neck, the muscles of which could be seen standing out like whipcord below the white cap.'[36]

James Billington (1847-1901) was the best man for the job. Quick and humane to those about to die, he was proud of his expertise

---

36 This rare, graphic detail about the broken neck was published in the *Hampshire Advertiser*, 19 July 1899.

and his tally of 151 executions. Although he had the air of a plain working-man, he had some strange places in his mind. At the age of eleven, he built a replica gallows, made dummies and practised hanging them. He was very strong, and implacable: most people were putty in his hands.

The black flagstaff was fixed on the high water-tower at 7 o'clock in the evening, and it was quickly seen, with a crowd gathering and gazing fixedly at it, until dusk came and they all dispersed. Around this time, a member of the press had the bright idea of routing out another official who had had some contact with Mary Ann.[37] This was Mr W Mandin, the county police court missionary (i.e. a person employed to attend the court to work for the spiritual and moral benefit of those brought before it). At first he was reluctant to speak, but eventually agreed, in, as he put it, the interests of truth. It would, however, have been better if he had kept his inexpert opinions to himself.

He said that he had spoken to Mary Ann several times before sentence of death was passed. 'Candidly,' he pronounced, 'I do not think she was insane. In all my dealings with her I have come to the conclusion that her demeanour was more sullen than anything else. I have seen the parents, and the father emphatically denies that there is insanity in the family. As to the murdered sister, Caroline, the father said that 'she was as right as you until her brother was killed, and then she fretted so much that her mind gave way.'" Sullenness is not a diagnosis. The comments about what the father said were grossly out of date; James came to know better as the case proceeded frighteningly and had long ago abandoned his protestations about the mental health of the Ansell family. He had faced up to the reality of 'imbecility'. Dr Forbes Winslow's report had been read to him. Family pride was nothing compared with execution. Theoretically, the missionary's dangerous and ill-considered remarks could have tipped the balance in the Home Secretary's final deliberations overnight when Mary Ann was on the threshold of death, but he had no intention of turning on the brink.

37 This was, in fact, a representative of the Press Association.

Night fell over the gloomy, waiting prison. Late, the chaplain visited Mary Ann. She knelt to pray, and slept fitfully. So did those others who cared about her, and those who worried that they had not done or said enough to save her.

CHAPTER ELEVEN

THE EMBLEM OF DEATH

At 6 o'clock in the morning, on Wednesday, July 19th, a warder was despatched to the post office to check if there was a telegram from the Home Office. Of course, there was none. The prisoner rose from the illusory safety of her bed and was helped to wash and dress. She was offered breakfast, but could eat very little. At 7 am, the chaplain came to comfort her and stayed at her side. Someone, probably the Chief Warder, told her that all hope was lost. What was going on was supposed to be secret and private, but Mr Lloyd, who was for some reason Acting Governor at this time, was reported as giving out a modicum of information afterwards.[38] If that is true, one would have thought that he risked his job.

Just before 8 o'clock, Mary Ann saw the face of the hangman. Billington had no assistant, not anticipating trouble. He entered swiftly and pinioned her arms behind her with a leather strap. The route to the place of execution was, unusually, not a direct one: the condemned woman was brought by female warders to the lodge at the entrance to the women's portion of the prison and delivered over to male warders for the last walk to the scaffold, which was in the van shed, near the laundry, just inside the courtyard behind the main gates. The ghastly archaic procession escorted the pinioned prisoner, with Mr Lloyd in his Governor's guise and the wan-faced chaplain in his robes behind. His presence was still a comfort as

---

38 Indeed, the *Manchester Evening News* carried a short statement: 'A *London Star* correspondent telegraphs that he is informed by the Governor of the Gaol that Mary Ansell has left behind a confession of her crime.'

he prayed, reading the Burial Service, a custom which was to be stopped in 1927, as causing too much anguish to the condemned. He had done his duty well – his charge had a contrite heart and every word that she uttered, as she was supported, not dragged, not carried, was a sign of her repentance. She was sobbing and praying all the way, if the reports were strictly true, and is supposed to have lamented, 'Oh, my God in Heaven' and 'Lord have mercy on my soul'. An alternative version is, 'O God! O Heaven! O Lord, forgive me.' She did not call for her parents: she had made her peace with them. She stood firmly on the scaffold as her legs were strapped and the hood and noose slipped on, and she could still hear the voice of the chaplain until the moment when she dropped 7 feet, and was killed instantly. It was only a minute and a half since she had left the female lodge, alive.

'Two men who stood close against the prison wall said that they distinctly heard the groans of the condemned girl, followed immediately by a thud, which told them plainly that the bolt had been drawn.' (*Hemel Hempstead Gazette*, July 22nd.) No press were allowed at the execution. The official witnesses, obliged to observe the whole proceedings, were the Under-Sheriff, the Sheriff's Officer and his clerk, the Chief Warder, three male warders, the Chaplain, and the Medical Officer, Dr Lipscombe. The doctor checked that life was extinct. The body was suspended for one hour, and was then removed for further medical examination and made decent for viewing.

By eerie coincidence, at 8 o'clock that morning, a postman brought a parcel to Mrs Sarah Ball, of Upper Tulse Hill, South London. It was, in effect, a legacy from Mary Ann – the beads which she used to wear around her neck. There was an accompanying letter from her: 'I am very pleased to tell you I have prayed to my God for pardon, and I am going to the Holy Communion on Wednesday before the fatal event takes place.' Mrs Ball revealed a previous simple letter from Mary Ann; 'I hope and trust all of you are in good health. I myself is as well as can be expect by this time. I cant think of any news now so please excuse a short letter.'

Unusual activity outside the red-brick prison began quietly on the fine summer's morning. The very high-walled building had some characteristics of an asylum, with its towers and chimneys, Governor's house and large, lofty chapel. The local journalists turned up for the event, and the hostile *Pall Mall Gazette* sent a journalist to cover the scene. When he arrived at 7 am, there were only three persons waiting, but as time went on, the crowd increased, with children flocking in their hundreds, and cyclists stopping on the bridge.

> The crowd was not of the motley description so common at Newgate on such occasions; it was composed of a better class of spectators, anxious, for the first time, apparently, to be present at the hoisting of the black flag, but withal they somehow seemed to fear to look upon the tell-tale flagstaff. It was noticeable, however, throughout, that the sympathy which so oftentimes accompanies a criminal to the scaffold was conspicuous only by its absence, for only on one or two occasions did I hear a murmur against the justice of the sentence meted out to the unhappy girl. A few minutes before eight the flagstaff ropes were seen to be in motion; the crowd gathered closer to the walls of the prison, and precisely at two minutes after the hour the black flag went slowly up amid breathless silence.

The *Daily Mail* disliked the spectacle:

> The hanging drew a crowd of several hundred people – children, youths, girls, working men, women with children in their arms, and a large proportion of the loafers of the town, who congregated with the morbid desire of seeing the death-flag rise from the prison walls. One or two sublimely hopeful persons suggested that a reprieve might even at the last moment arrive by telegraph, but the crowd had the morning's paper in its hands, and scouted the notion of a reprieve. A few minutes before eight the cords of the flagstaff were shaken by an invisible hand, and populace, policemen, and City people waiting on the platform for their train looked up and waited silently. A moment later the lines moved again and the black flag crept above the tower coping and slowly unfolded itself in the breeze. At nine o'clock the emblem of death was withdrawn.

Apparently, a few men removed their hats as the flag went up, and some people were kneeling and praying in the road. The railway bridge in Victoria Street was jammed with onlookers, and others were watching from nearby allotments. From 7.45, for a quarter of an hour, the bell was tolling the death knell at St Peter's Church, and in due course, the sum of two and sixpence was paid for the bell-ringer's services. Bets were laid for a reprieve. One man climbed a telegraph pole on the embankment, but was ordered down by a constable. (The *Hertfordshire Advertiser*, *passim*, which had run its own campaign to save Mary Ansell.) The *Watford Observer* estimated that the crowd numbered nearly 2,000 and was very orderly. Agents of the Religious Tract Society distributed their leaflets liberally, and at the end the words, 'She is gone' rose up like a Common Prayer.

Earlier, not long ago, there had been Caroline's inquest, but now, two hours after the execution, Mary Ann's own inquest was to take place. The appointed jurors – 13 answered to their names when they were called – arrived punctually at 10 o'clock at the huge gates of the prison. The worst duty – to view the body – came first, and then the hearing took place in a small, inner room. It was quite short, and very formal, formulaic, even. Only after a tense altercation were the press allowed in, and, in fact, the resulting shorthand notes provided a valuable record, which would otherwise have been absent. Reporters had been resolutely excluded from the execution, although the custom was, then, that most prisons generally did admit them in the case of *male* hangings. Some of the newspapers had objected, on the grounds that secrecy did not sit well with a disputed case, *especially* a young woman.

Edward Lloyd, the Chief Warder, summarised the main events, and identified the body. 'Everything, I suppose, was carried out in a satisfactory way?' the Coroner, Dr Lovell Drage, asked. 'In a most satisfactory way, sir.' Mr James Stephen Hand, juror, 'Was death instantaneous?' Chief Warder: 'Yes, quite so. There was not a movement of any kind.' Coroner: 'Then you are able to say that the deceased was duly executed according to law?' Chief Warder: 'Yes.' The prison doctor, Dr Eustace Henry Lipscombe, stated, 'I have seen the deceased woman every day since her sentence and frequently before. I was present this morning when the execution was carried out. The person was Mary Ann Ansell. Death was due to dislocation of the vertebral column, between the first and second cervical vertebrae. I believe death was instantaneous. There was no movement or struggle of any kind.'

Mr Richard Samuel, juror, invited to examine the doctor, asked a question which reflected the public anxiety about Mary Ann's mental state: 'I should like to ask the doctor what has been the general conduct or demeanour of the girl since the sentence.'

Coroner, swiftly knocking him back: 'I think that is scarcely within the purview of this inquest.'

Samuel, withdrawing: 'I am sorry to have asked the question.'

Then they buried the body of Mary Ann Ansell in a shell, in quicklime, within the precincts of the prison, as the law required. Her grave was no. 2, and she was the last woman to be hanged in Hertfordshire.

⚜

The story was far from over. Revelations and consequences, defences and accusations accrued, as they do after a shattering event. It turned out that the Chaplain, well known to be traumatised by the whole affair, was, additionally under an official cloud. His son, the Press Association had reported on July 19th, had made a statement that the vexed interview, seen and resented by the Home Office, which had appeared in the *Daily Mail*, was 'quite unauthorised' and had been considerably 'amplified' by the newspaper. 'My father,' said the son, 'does not deny or support the interview, because he is responsible only to the Home Office.'

The *Daily Mail* commented, now, on July 20th:

> This is a somewhat remarkable statement, coming at this time. The interview with our representative, in which the Chaplain expressed his opinion as to the girl's mental and moral condition and her incapability of understanding the nature of her crime, was given some ten days ago, and it is singular that this statement should only have appeared yesterday. It will be noted of course that the accuracy of the interview is not denied. It is only stated to be "unauthorised" and "amplified". We understand that the Chaplain was informed by the Home Office that he ought not to have made any

> such communication. He made no statement yesterday as to what
> the condemned girl said or did during his last interview with her.

Obviously, reprimanded and embarrassed, overcome by the reality of 'an eye for an eye', the Chaplain was not going to open up to any journalist. In fact, the entire, quite plausible version of the conduct of the preamble to the execution, widely accepted, may all have been guesswork, and the Chief Warder may not have 'leaked' any information at all. Rumours of Mary Ann's utter collapse did circulate.

The Home Office itself was disconcerted on the day after the execution when, very late, too late, Mary Ann's birth certificate, as ordered, arrived from Scotland Yard. For some reason, Sergeant George Lambert had not made a search at Somerset House until that precise day. The details of the certificate reveal that Mary Ann Ansell, born on November 18th, 1877, was only twenty-one years old when she was hanged. Somehow, this true age makes her seem significantly younger. Neither Mary Ann herself, nor her own mother remembered her birth date, although her birth was registered.

The revised age meant that the carefully inscribed '22' on all the inquest papers, and others relating to the death, where correct identification was paramount, was an inaccuracy. Perfect satisfaction had eluded the Home Office. Therefore, a notice of amendment was inserted in the newspapers on July 26th:

> In reference to statements which have appeared to the effect that
> Mary Ann Ansell, who was executed last week, was only 18 years of
> age, we are informed that she stated in evidence that she was 22, and
> that subsequently on inquiry at Somerset House it was ascertained
> that she was born in November, 1877, and was consequently in her
> 22nd year when the crime was committed.

This was subtly slanted: by the time of the hanging, few people thought that Mary Ann was only 18, and by the use of 'in her 22nd year' the actual age of 21 was not emphasised.

The *St Albans Gazette*, transcribing the above official notice, went on to say: 'We are asked to contradict the many false statements that have been circulated respecting the condemned girl's condition at the time of the execution. While she was naturally unnerved and sobbed piteously, she bore up throughout the trying ordeal with astonishing bravery, and walked to the scaffold practically without assistance. The idea that she was "dragged to the drop" appears to be purely apocryphal.'

The notice also contained the new information that 'before the execution she made a full confession of the crime and of the motive which prompted it.' The general public were not aware that the Home Office, as we have seen, already held on to the secret of the confession to the Broadmoor doctors. It was traditional that the State liked to have a confession to 'justify' a hanging, and the powerful Church, also, required its clergy to encourage a confession. On July 20th, *after* the execution, now that hope of reprieve was irrelevant, the Acting Matron of St Albans prison, EA Whyte, sat down and wrote a letter to the Governor:

> Sir, I beg to submit to you as requested the following statement made by the prisoner to me. I was sitting with Ansell during the breakfast hour on Sunday the 16th inst. She was crying bitterly, and said, Matron I must tell you. If I die next Wednesday, I deserve my fate. I did send the cake to my poor Carry.
>
> I said shall I give you some papers, so that you can write down all you wish and you may send it to the Governor or Chaplain yourself. She asked, do you mean write a confession? Yes. Oh no I could not write one now but I will confess all to the Chaplain, and my father too, but oh how shall I ask my father to forgive me? I answered her, her father could not hold his forgiveness, and it would be the right thing to do. I then asked her when she conceived the idea of taking her sister's life, before or after the insurance was effected? She replied, Oh before, but not until Mr Cooper had again and again worried me to insure somebody, I wanted the money to get things, to get married, and my young man could not give me much, and poor Carry was no good to anybody.

The Home Secretary saw this document on July 20th, and copies were sent to the two examining doctors, and to Judge Mathew, but the contents were not generally released. No one had a field-day, but there was plenty of official satisfaction.

It was the Reverend Henry Fowler who had the most bitter task, and crisis of conscience. He, too, wrote to the Governor on July 20th:

> Sir, I desire to state that on Monday July 17th, I put the question in the most solemn manner to the prisoner Mary Ann Ansell whether she was guilty of the crime for which she was condemned and the taking away the life of her sister. She answered without demur "Yes, and it was bad company" (which was the cause.)

This kind and honourable man, who had daughters of his own, had stayed silent, and had not faltered in his ministrations. It was awkward for him that Mary Ann's words did not entirely accord with his previous opinion of her mental responsibility, for which he had been offensively – we cannot doubt – castigated. We cannot know if he had taken advice from a senior cleric about the confidentiality of the confession, but he had certainly delayed his revelation. As for the 'bad company', this is the first and last such reference. She may have meant her young man only, although the words conjure up a gang of unsuitable companions. It is disturbing that she has expressed two different reasons or motives for her actions; one, to furnish the imagined marriage, and the other, egged on, for unspecified financial gain. It makes her seem like a fantasist.

An individual who was thinking entirely of himself and his reputation, and was seeking to distance himself from the shriller parts of the Ansell protest, was Dr Forbes Winslow. On the actual day of the execution, he wrote unfeelingly to Sir Matthew White Ridley:

> Now that this case has been dealt with I would like to give you my position in the matter which you probably know. I was called in for an urgent written opinion in the same way as Counsel might, with facts, affidavits placed before me (not as an agitator). The solicitor for the defence consulted me on July 9th, requesting me to apply for permission to see the girl. I informed him that this would not be granted. I was then wired to send you a Report which I did. I have taken no further part in the public agitation – beyond what I here state and which was my professional duty to do.' Sincerely, Forbes Winslow.

Another informant who had held her fire until after the execution was Ada Anne Whiddington, headmistress of Manchester Street School. She wrote on July 23rd to the *Daily Chronicle*:

> I have made no declaration whatever about the unfortunate girl, and I am in no way responsible for statements made by a late assistant or late caretaker. I kept silence merely because I wished the poor girl to have every chance of a reprieve. Mary Ansell entered my class in 1885, and passed steadily from the lowest class to the highest. She was examined at the end of each year by Her Majesty's Inspector, and received a certificate for passing the examination. I have looked through my examination schedules and find that in the five successive years she was examined she never failed in any one subject. After Mary Ansell had gained a certificate for passing the Fifth Standard she left, or she would undoubtedly have passed the Sixth and Seventh Standards successfully. In the face of these facts I could not say that she was possessed of defective intellect during her five years' stay in this school. As I remember her she was as sane as her sister, who is at present time working in my Sixth Standard. It is very possible, I think, that people may be mixing her up with her poisoned sister or another sister of seventeen, who is weak in intellect and has fits.

This girl cannot be the right Mary Ann Ansell. Mrs Whiddington's academic achiever is not the Mary Ann whose slovenly, slanting handwriting, lack of punctuation, poor grammar and spelling we are familiar with. The required standard must have been higher than this. Moreover, the headmistress's account lacks the telling personal details which are provided by the other staff and are consistent withal. The indications are that Mrs Whiddington from Limerick has no anecdotal material to hand, and that she does not actually remember Mary Ann. She does not even use the full name, while those who did know her were careful to identify her by her two Christian names. Looking up old records might not have been precise, because Ansell was a common name in the district. A possible source of confusion might have been that Mary Ann Ansell's first cousin, Mary Ann Rowley (Harriett Parish's sister) born in 1870, was also a pupil at Manchester Street from 1879.

Mrs Whiddington's condescending attitude towards lower status staff may have some connection with her desire to write to the press and assert her authority. Is it possible, too, that her memory was not very good, even though she now held the post of Head? Research has brought up the surprising fact that she suffered a serious head injury at the age of 30, in 1891, when she was a teacher at Manchester Street. On November 11th, there was a great gale. Walking to work, and just outside the gates, she was hit by a flying chimney pot, and taken, unconscious, to the nearby Royal Free Hospital in Gray's Inn Road. Severe injuries to her head were found, but the wards were full and she had to be sent home to recover.

Searching in her mind for 'imbecile' girls who might have been taken for Mary Ann by her muddled colleagues, she nominates poor Caroline herself, and also Martha, the seventeen-year old on the waiting list for Leavesden in 1899. The trouble with Caroline is that Board School records, to hand, show that, as already mentioned, Caroline was never a pupil at Manchester Street although all the other siblings, including Martha, are clearly listed there. First born, in 1873, Manchester Street had not yet opened when, aged four, she was ready for school. She could have attended St Peter's National School in Dutton Street.

As for the suggestion that Martha was the strange and difficult girl, the age gap is too great. There were five years between them, and that, in the context of school, is a world apart. Both Caroline and Martha were known epileptics. Mary Ann was not. Epilepsy is a conspicuous disability. How could the staff have mixed them up with Mary Ann?

The discrepancy between Mrs Whiddington's paragon and 'Silly Old Ansell' is so bizarre that it has to be challenged. The affidavits of the Molonys amply corroborate the versions of the teacher, Mrs GW Ayres, and the caretaker, both of whom were willing to swear affidavits.

Disquiet about the execution still seethed, and on the following Saturday, July 22nd, a well-attended public meeting, with the Marquess of Queensberry present, was held in the large hall of the Freemasons' Tavern to protest at the 'too hasty' hanging, and to support a proposal for the formation of a Court of Criminal Appeal. Mr RD Yelverton, consumed by doubt and suspicions about the case, reckless about his reputation in the eyes of the Establishment, took the chair and spoke for over one and a half hours. He traversed the entire history, and contended that the girl had never confessed. He said that he had it on good authority from a friend in St Albans that that was the situation and he challenged the Government to produce any such document. (Cheers.) It was a shameful thing that such stories should be published when the dead girl had no chance of refuting them. Mary Ann Ansell had never been proved guilty; her examination by Dr Nicolson, of Broadmoor, was not the thing, because he was not an independent expert. (Hear! Hear!) It was time the minions of the Government were prevented from shutting their mouths at the bidding of a Prime Minister. Sir Matthew White Ridley had sent to her account a woman who was, at all events, argumentatively insane, and had not been proved to commit the crime with which she was charged. The whole thing was a terrible one, and nothing short of judicial murder. The stopping of the Cannon Street meeting (he alleged) was due to Governmental interference.

The resolutions were adopted, one seconded by loyal Mr Jobson, still earnest and active. A second protest had been planned for the following afternoon, Sunday, in Trafalgar Square, but Mr Jobson had not given sufficient legal notice to the authorities. He was always being thwarted. The widely reported Saturday meeting caused some consternation:

> Before Mr RD Yelverton appeared on the scene, [the *Hertfordshire Gazette* complained on July 26th] everyone believed the unfortunate girl was proved guilty of murder. This gentleman, however, has discovered, to his own satisfaction, at any rate, that the evidence given at the trial will not hold water. Probably, though it is difficult to say, by this time he is sorry he spoke as he did on Saturday.

The Home Office kept their own counsel, grimly, but, in spite of Mr Yelverton's opinions on *Ansell*, he was a force to be reckoned with in the establishment of the Court of Criminal Appeal, the cause to which he devoted himself.

CHAPTER TWELVE

'UNDER A CURSE'

The Chaplain was dead in less than one year and it may well have been that he did not recover from his protracted ordeal. Although the notion had spread that he was an infirm 80-year-old on the brink of the grave, the truth is that he was only 73 years of age when he died at home, without warning, on Sunday, May 20th, 1900. Born, like Mary Ann in Bloomsbury, but in a more agreeable part, the Reverend Henry Fowler, an Oxford man, Exeter College, was a scholar, and an antiquarian, the author of *The Wall of the Monastery of St Albans*. A sensitive and dutiful person, he was drawn to the poor and to those in trouble.

After early curacies and a spell as second master at St Albans Grammar School, he settled in the old Roman town and was Chaplain at the workhouse from 1865 to 1895, while concurrently chaplain at the prison from 1880 onwards. He was not a solitary, studious cleric, but had a considerable family of his own to maintain. With his wife, Julia Frances, he had (by 1881) six sons and two daughters, but Julia died on September 21st, 1885. Of necessity, there were always servant girls in the house, and, therefore, he was used to their ways and conversation. On his last day, he had conducted a service at the prison chapel. When his family returned from church in the evening, they found him dead. Two sons, Cecil and Hugh, were away in South Africa, serving their country in the Boer War.

The scarcely begun career of Percy Wisbey had not been enhanced by the disastrous Ansell case, and he did not prosper, although he should have been admired for the way in which he picked himself up and fought to save his client. Mary Ann was often described journalistically as friendless and alone, but those words seem better to attach to her young lawyer. There is no impression that, in practice on his own account, he had access to a community of older and wiser lawyers. He found himself in the intolerable position of being repeatedly called to account in the public forum, being asked to explain what had gone wrong, where a more experienced man would have been more circumspect. He tried to rationalise the conduct of the trial, while preserving correct etiquette about his barrister's input. His versions tended to vary somewhat. He was unsupported: Clarke Hall did not stand shoulder to shoulder with him, and that would not have been expected of him. The barrister would not have regarded him highly, a small, provincial solicitor, right out in the sticks, not used to big cases, with no background, not from Oxford or Cambridge, not a member of a large, successful firm, and that was the way it was – a social and professional divide.

Percy Wisbey had too many sadnesses in his short life. He was born in October, 1876, one year before Mary Ann, at 33 Acacia Road, St John's Wood, London, to Charles Wordsworth Wisbey and Marianita (Hopkins). In 1881, his eldest brother, Walpole, died at the age of 15, and in 1883, the father died in Brighton. In 1891, Percy and his mother were living in Lancaster Road, Kensington, and the plan was that Percy would become a solicitor. A record of his passing his preliminary Law Society Examination in 1893 has been found, and he qualified between that year and the Ansell case in 1899. He had moved out of London to Hemel Hempstead with his mother and his other brother, Charles Henry, born in 1874. He did enter into a brief partnership with one Harold Mee, but the *Law Journal*, 1901 (volume 35, p64) recorded that the partnership, practising at Hemel Hempstead under the style of Percy Wisbey and Co. had been dissolved. Harold Mee, son of a Birmingham hardware merchant, the same age as Percy, appears in the 1901 Census living in Birmingham.

The Wisbey family was exotic, with foreign elements and diverse talents. Marianita, Percy's mother, was born in Santa Anna, Columbia,

South America. Her father, Evan Hopkins, FGS, was an engineer, author of *On the Connexion of Geology with Terrestrial Magnetism* (1843). Hopkins lived adventurously in Africa as a surveyor, with connections to proposed railways, and the managements of gold mines – at which he had varied success. Percy's father, born in Chelsea in 1838, was a civil servant, a clerk in the War Office. His father, Charles Watling Wisbey, had been a 'Public Political Writer'. Percy's father left a substantial personal estate to his own mother, not to his children. There were family mysteries. Percy's eldest brother was dead. Percy never seemed to have much money. Charles Henry (Harry) at one stage a student for the Bar, held multiple posts as a schoolmaster and coach, and taught in South Africa and Smyrna, where he was headmaster at the British School. Finally he was admitted to the Bar (Middle Temple) in 1919, and he was a Fellow of the Royal Geographical Society.

A chance of happiness came to Percy Wisbey when, in 1902, he married Violet Absolon, in Epsom, Surrey. Violet's grandfather was John Absolon (1815-1895) a well-known artist – painter of seascape, landscape and genre in both oil and watercolour. Violet's father, Arthur de Mansfield Absolon, was a bank clerk. In 1903, Percy and Violet abandoned Hemel Hempstead and moved to Portsmouth, where he practised on his own account in Commercial Road. Local newspapers report a number of small cases, mostly in the magistrates' courts, where he defended hopeless cases, and usually lost. In that year, a daughter, Dorothy Violet, was born in Southsea. In need of more money, no doubt, Percy tried being an employed solicitor, not realising, perhaps that his new principal, the famous London criminal solicitor, Arthur Newton, who was deeply involved in the Cleveland Street brothel scandal and the trial of Oscar Wilde, and, later, Crippen, had a dubious reputation: he did eventually come to grief. Percy found himself in a challenging environment, with professional criminals and members of High Society as clients, not to mention worldly, more sophisticated colleagues. Was *Ansell* ever discussed? Very ordinary cases were assigned to him; they sent him off to places like Sheffield, and Derby. However, his time was limited:

on June 1st, 1909, he died at Fountain Cottage, Ashtead, Surrey, aged 32, the cause of death Pulmonary Tuberculosis and Syncope. He bequeathed £332 13s 6d to his wife, Violet, and she found a job as a maternity nurse, working for a family in North Kensington in 1911. It was a sad ending to her marriage. She began to visit America, taking her daughter with her. In 1940, aged 58, a widow, she was managing a hospital ward in New Jersey.

The two Leavesden doctors are not likely to have been affected by the execution. Dr Blair did abandon an asylum career for greater achievement in the world at large, but that decision undoubtedly came from his temperament and ambitions. In 1901, he surfaces as one of the pioneers in laying the foundation of Northern Nigeria, serving there first as Assistant Medical Officer. Nigeria, its people and its government became the passion of his life. He was appointed Senior Medical Officer in 1907, and later Senior Sanitary Officer.

> In his job he was singularly fortunate....It was his business to inspect and advise on the sites of all Government stations. The whole of the Protectorate thus became his province. In the course of his journeyings he acquired a knowledge of the country that can scarcely have been rivalled. Travelling in days before the advent of motor-cars, his method of progressing was almost invariably on foot. His horses were led behind him, but seldom carried more than empty saddles. The distances that he covered in this fashion were enormous. There was hardly a village or wayside market which at some time or other he had not visited. Nor was there any place where, after a single visit, his return was not hailed with acclamations. For Blair had the instinctive faculty of winning the confidence of the natives, who were quick to perceive his transparent kindness of heart.... Among his colleagues in the Nigerian Service, it is safe to say that no man was more universally loved. He knew them all....To many a lonely District Officer the sight of Blair's sunburnt, spectacled, heavy-mustachioed visage, as he strode into a bush-station was the most welcome moment in the year's tour of service.'[39]

He died in January, 1933. His brother, Dr David Blair had remained in the asylum world, becoming Medical Superintendent of the Lancashire County Mental Hospital at Prestwich.

39 *The Times*, January 21st, 1933.

Dr Elkins dug in behind the yellow and red walls of Leavesden and flourished. In the year after the murder he brought in a wife who was happy to join him there. Caroline Peach, whose father was a farmer, of Waingroves Hall, Derbyshire, was 29 years old, and the doctor was 38. She had been a governess before being rescued for a fuller life. The wedding, on April 19th, 1900, embodied all that was loyal and cohesive about the old asylum communities. It took place at All Saints' Church, Leavesden, and the asylum chaplain, the Reverend JRB Watson, officiated, assisted by the Reverend Arthur Wilson, vicar of the parish.

The bridegroom left his residence at 2 pm, amid the cheers of the officials and the patients. He was popular. A surprise had been prepared: as he passed through the gates of the institution in his carriage, all the children from the nearby St Pancras Industrial School were waiting there to give him a send-off. The school, where orphaned and street children were trained as apprentices and domestic servants, had a close relationship with the asylum, and was designed by the same architect.

The horses slowed to a walk, and the school band paraded in front down Asylum Road, playing a wedding march. The bride, known as Lena, was dressed in silver-grey. The church was a blaze of colour, with banks of potted plants from the asylum gardeners supplementing the Easter decorations. Afterwards, children lining the path-way threw flowers. Later, Dr and Mrs Elkins left for their honeymoon in Ilfracombe, Devonshire. In the evening, the asylum staff held a celebration dance in the recreation hall. There were three children of the marriage, and no doubt they thrived as such children usually did in their singular environment. Robert Francis Elkins became a Commander of the Royal Navy.

Dr Elkins' benevolent side shows in an obituary, written by him, in the 'Leavesden Asylum Magazine' (September, 1904): 'We have committed to his last resting place a well-known character in the institution, William Jewell, commonly known as "Billy" or "Snatcher". He was a great favourite, always willing to do anything for anyone. As church-warden he was most energetic, and took the greatest interest in a stranger coming to officiate. "Billy" was a firm believer in hand-shaking. No one must omit that ceremony, from the Bishop downwards. Last year, when the Bishop of Colchester arrived, "Billy" was ready to receive his lordship with outstretched hand and "How do, Mr Colchester." What a life! Born in Shoreditch Workhouse, lived there for forty years, and thirty-one years in Leavesden.'

During the war, retired to Hormead, Parkside Drive, Watford, Dr Elkins died on September 10th, 1941. Probate was granted to his widow, and he left the goodly sum of £1,136 9s.

Dr Forbes Winslow did not lose sleep over the Ansell case, and, anyway, he was constantly seeing patients and their relatives. At the time, he was just a trifle anxious that he might have appeared to have over-over-stepped the mark. He had never even met the girl; she was one more unfortunate to him, wrongly condemned, with his expert advice unheeded yet again. He was used to it, and so was his father before him. Mary Ann made a useful contribution to his *Recollections*, where the illustrations of familial imbecility spoke for themselves, he thought, and his sage and scientific observations palpably should have prevailed after the trial. Besides, he was preoccupied with his British Hospital for Mental Disorders (Forbes Winslow Memorial) which he had founded in 1890, and also with the writing of his three tomes on insanity. He died suddenly from heart failure at 57 Devonshire Street, on June 8th, 1913, in his seventieth year.

One person who actually benefitted from the Ansell case, his most important murder, was Superintendent Wood. His fine detective work in Leavesden and Bloomsbury, and, especially, his preparation for court, were recognised, and aided his career. He was promoted to Superintendent at Watford, and was in post for twenty-two years. In 1911, he was appointed Deputy Chief Constable. He held the King's Police Medal and he was awarded the OBE. After retirement in 1920, he died at the age of 66 in 1925. He was a Scotsman, the son of an Aberdeenshire farmer. When interviewed in 1920, he said of Mary Ann Ansell, 'Mr Clarke Hall made a magnificent attempt to save her life at the Assizes.' 'Ever since I was raised to the position of Superintendent,' he went on, 'I have tried to use that position for doing what good I could among the poor. I always believed in helping the under-dog, and have often found that a little kindness goes an astonishingly long way, even with well-known convicts as well as with first offenders.' He supported, *inter alia*, the Society for Improving the Condition of the Watford Poor, and the NSPCC.

The most tragic survivors of the disaster were the depleted Ansell family members huddled at no 1 Tankerton Street, with James out hunting for work, and the landlord calling for his rent. The married couple might have seemed like 'the old folk' to reporters, but people had lost sight of the fact that there were very young children to care for. Aged as she looked, Sarah had given birth to Frederick the year before the execution, and William, born in 1895, and John, born in 1892, were not much older. Every charitable benefit for which the Ansells were eligible will have come to them, and the equally impoverished neighbours did what they could. There was no stigma attached and they were not shunned.

In 1901, Martha (18) had not yet been removed to Leavesden, Emma, the useful, literate girl, her father's prop, aged 16, was working as a sweet maker, and, therefore, at last, there was someone other than James, then a bricklayer's labourer, to bring in a financial contribution. Louisa (14) and Florence (12) were at home and the three little boys were all there. By 1908, after so many years at Tankerton Street, the family had moved to 5 Ossulston Place, in Somerstown, where there had long been relatives, particularly the Rowley family at 43 Ossulston Street. The two families were close. James's sister, Mary Ann Ansell, aunt and namesake of James and Sarah's Mary Ann, was the woman who had married John Rowley, a hawker of baskets and mats, and given birth to five living children, including Mary Ann Rowley and Harriett Rowley (later Parish).

In 1911, James was still a 'general labourer', Louisa (24) was improving as a shop girl, and John (16) was a 'general porter'. The household was becoming more solvent. Martha was long gone to the asylum. Emma, Florence, William and Frederick were not present for the census, but Sarah had a new child to look after – Florence Ansell, her four-year-old granddaughter, whose parentage is not clear. She could have been her daughter, Florence's, illegitimate child. Florence had had a statedly illegitimate child, named Martha Louise Ansell, in 1910. That child died in Great Ormond Street Hospital on February 3rd, 1911, her home address 5 Ossulston Place. Whooping cough and sequelae, with convulsions had caused the death. Florence married Thomas Coy, a mineral water worker, in 1910. A son, John, was born to them in 1911, and a daughter, Louise Ellen, in 1914. However, Sarah's granddaughter, Florence, is not listed as a member of the Coy family. In 1914, Thomas Coy died at St Pancras Infirmary.

James and Sarah Ansell moved again, not far, in 1915, to 59 Stibbington Street, later Chalton Street, shown to Charles Booth, social reformer, author of works such as *Old Age Pensions and the Aged Poor* (1899) as one of the worst poverty spots in London. Widowed Florence was living with them. That street is where Sarah Ansell died, aged 65, on March 13th, 1916, during the Great War, when food was beginning to get short and the poorest at home suffered the most. The cause of death was heart failure, with bronchitis and senility. James was now a pensioned Gas Company Labourer. *Deo gratias!*

Emma Ansell moved back in with her widowed father, and they were both together at number 59 Stibbington Street in 1918 and 1921. Emma, in 1922, was joined by her brother, Frederick, but James was no longer there. Dementia, not insanity, must have supervened, and he had been removed to Banstead Mental Hospital as it was known by then. Founded in Surrey in 1877 as a Lunatic Asylum, it was never a designated 'Imbecile Asylum'. There he died on July 25th, 1928, aged 76, the informant F (Frederick) Ansell, son, of 59 Stibbington Street. The cause of death was cardiovascular degeneration, with no post-mortem ordered, certified by AAW Petrie. After years of toil and anxiety, James was cared for at the end.

Kindness and leniency are small illuminations in the Ansells' existence. 'Clemency for a woman of sorrows' had come to Mrs Sarah Ansell at the Highgate Police Court on Monday, April 28th, 1902. She had been arrested on the Sunday night, and charged with being drunk and disorderly: she was found, quite incapable, lying on the footway in Archway Road. She was in deep mourning, and her face was 'much damaged' (probably by scrofula). She could not stop sobbing as she tried to explain that she had had a lot of trouble with her children: one poisoned, another hanged, another killed in a railway accident, and a fourth recently removed to a lunatic asylum. Her husband earned only 26 shillings a week, and the rent was 6s/6d. The drinking episode came over her after visiting Highgate Cemetery where a niece had just been buried. It was all too much for her. She knew that she was guilty, and she was very sorry.

The magistrate, Mr Reynolds, said that he recognised her and was very sorry to see her before him. 'The last time I saw you was when your unfortunate daughter was sentenced to death. God knows you have had enough trouble, Mrs Ansell. I hope this won't occur again: you are discharged.' The prisoner thanked him tearfully and left the court with her daughter and son-in-law.

An *Express* reporter picked up the unusual story, and made his way to the Ansells' 'wretched home' in Tankerton Street. 'We seem to be under a curse,' Sarah Ansell said. Her husband took over: 'As long as I can find work I can struggle on; but I'm getting on in life, and it is the young man who gets the pick of the jobs.'

It was brought up from time to time in Hertfordshire newspapers that one of Mary Ann Ansell's brothers had confessed to Caroline's murder on his deathbed. A gallant move, but it shows that the crime had preyed on his mind and caused collateral damage. It is, of course, impossible for any brother to have been guilty of the crime, because in 1899 there was no living brother of sufficient age. John, William and Frederick were seven, four and two respectively.

Hopefully, no one told the family that a waxwork effigy of Mary Ann had been made with speed in 1899 and was being exhibited in that year. Her figure could be viewed for two pence at Stewart's Grand Waxworks, High Street, Edinburgh, together with a live American Bearded Lady, and a company of trained performing cockatoos. The description was, 'Mary Ansell, the London cake Poisoner.' No doubt, her familiar hat and cape had been copied (surely not the originals), and she looked frightening with her dark eyes and unfriendly expression. They had made a bogy-woman of her, as if she were Amelia Dyer or Kate Webster. The French newspaper, *Le Petit Parisien*, published on July 30th, 1899, an imaginary illustration (see cover) of the hanging of Mary Ansell. The open-air setting, the French gendarmes, be-wigged lawyers, and the height of the suspended, trussed figure are wrong in detail but capture the stark reality of the occasion.

Feelings of anxiety about the execution persisted while it was in living memory. Miss Ellen Hayes, for many years an Inspector of Prisons and therefore not likely to have been unduly sensitive, said in an article of 1923 that Mary Ann was 'undoubtedly insane' and that 'she had all the marks of imbecility about her.' In a terrible image, she describes how, 'I caught a glimpse of the poor creature as she was being hurried away, and the sight is one I shall never forget. The look on her face was that of the poor hunted animal being led to the slaughter. I was told afterwards that she had summoned to her aid a wonderful reserve of courage in the last few minutes and had met her death bravely enough.'

A reasonable prediction, based upon Mary Ann's worsening behaviour in her workplace, even if she had committed no crime, would have been that eventually she would join her two sisters at Leavesden. Whatever her mental status actually amounted to, Mary Ann Ansell was, once she had formed a fixed intent, a dangerous and deteriorating individual at large, and she should have been placed appropriately at Broadmoor Asylum. She was a spiteful person and her moral depth was shallow. Half a century later, the Homicide Act of 1957 would have sheltered her, acknowledging her diminished responsibility, and allowing her abnormality of mind to arise from a wide spectrum of causes or conditions.

In 1931, when the city council took over the prison, Mary Ann's remains were raised from the prison plot and reinterred in St Albans City Cemetery in an unmarked grave.

Poisoned Caroline still lies in the disused Leavesden Asylum Cemetery – the old, north one, thickly haunted, so it is said, accessible through a lych-gate – in an unknown grave. By the end of 1903, by a count, 5,090 bodies had been buried there, with space for only 156 more. Up to six coffins used to be placed in one communal grave. Another cemetery was consecrated in 1908, and has since been turned into woodland. Here, the coffins were piled up to 18ft deep, and the number varied from one to seventeen. This seems gruesome and lamentable, reminiscent of the wholesale burial of paupers in mass graves earlier in the nineteenth century, and inconsistent with the ideals of the model asylum as it was planned. Leavesden closed, after many changes, in 1995, and the site was, as usual, redeveloped for housing, with most of the ward blocks demolished and some token buildings such as the administrative section, with the most impressive architecture, and the chapel, preserved. To what are these relics a tribute, since the whole idea of the asylum is discredited? Some grudging feeling that they are, after all, of historical interest is there, and a sense that there should be a monument to the thousands of lives spent and lost inside the encircling walls.[40]

40 Feelings about the execution persisted while it was in living memory. Contemporary learned journals raked over the various issues. *The Law Magazine and Review* (1903) p. 24 criticised the refusal to allow Dr Forbes Winslow to see Mary Ann Ansell. *The Month: A Catholic Magazine* (July – December, 1899) thought that she was not shown to be responsible for her acts and proposed that a *médecin légiste*, or criminologist, should sit as assessor with the judge. *The Saturday Review* (22 July 1899) p. 95, criticised the secrecy of the tribunal 'if it can be so called' (i.e. the two Broadmoor doctors) and the way in which no reasons were disclosed for the ultimate decision. *The Lancet*, however, failed to see any mitigating circumstances. *The Journal of Mental Science* (October, 1899) also wholly supported the result of the trial: 'Of evidence of insanity on the part of the prisoner there was not a shred. It was said that she had several insane relatives, but this was denied by her father [an astonishing remark] and, even if it were the fact, it is utterly out of the question that every person with an insane heredity should be held immune from punishment. Such a practice would be intolerable, as well as most unjust. That a medical man should be found to express an "emphatic" opinion of the prisoner's irresponsibility is much to be regretted, but it is satisfactory to find that no alienist could be found to endorse that opinion' [a gross misrepresentation of the history of the case]. *Humanity* (Volume III, no 55, September, 1899) p. 164 argues that 'the crime itself indicates a feeble brain, a paltry mind, and the power of affection apparently quite undeveloped – a nature in fact as near to imbecility as may be.' (Edward Carpenter). *The Humane Review* (1901, Volume I) p. 68, saw the hanging as an example, but a valueless one: 'The Home Secretary demonstrated that he did not intend to exempt women from the law, and the day that the drop fell, in spite of all the ceaseless efforts to obtain a reprieve for that half-witted, semi-irresponsible murder she would be hanged – and yet within a few months Louise Masset murders her own boy!' (Manfred

Louis Masset, aged 3, her illegitimate child, found dead, hit and suffocated, on October 27th, 1899, in the women's lavatory at Dalston Junction railway station. Louise, a governess, was hanged at Newgate by James Billington on January 26th, 1900. Her motive remains unclear.) Note: Dr Charles Arthur Mercier (1852–1919) of 34 Wimpole Street, an alienist of solid reputation, physician for Mental Diseases to Charing Cross Hospital, author, experienced as medical officer at asylums, was the reporter on recent medico-legal cases for the *Journal of Mental Science* and he was clearly no admirer of Dr Forbes Winslow. Elsewhere in the report in the journal (supra) he names him as the sole alienist to be found to attest to insanity.

APPENDIX

Certain covert factors lay behind the reluctance to spare Mary Ann. Her mere occupation was an element that damned her. A lurking phobia about servants simmered in the Victorian psyche because in a few but notorious cases a maid had turned against her employer in a paroxysm of resentment, envy, greed, or an outbreak of insanity. In modern homes where a single maid was kept, the forced intimacy of sharing facilities could break down barriers of respect. Lone widows were especially nervous. Perfect maids and cook generals were becoming difficult to find. 'Sullenness' was rife. Kate Webster, who, in 1879, had boiled up the remains of her mistress in the kitchen copper, was a figure of nightmares. There was a feeling that servants alone in their kitchens, with potential poisons on their shelves, had to be watched, and bad ones stamped out.

Lesser known cases illustrate the public suspicion. At the same time as Ansell, another maid was being harried through the Hertfordshire courts. She was only fifteen, but the Crown was determined to charge that Leonora Ann Melinda Florence Robinson, of Watford, had caused atropine poison to be taken by Henry and Elizabeth Crawley and their four children with intent to murder them, on February 10th, 1899. Leonora worked all day for the Crawleys at 137 Queen's Road, Watford, and went home to her parents at 172 St Albans Road, at night. She had left the Bushey Village School in December, 1897, and, while a pupil there, had attended cookery classes. In her job, she gave every satisfaction, and there was even mutual affection.

This seems to have been a case of accident, with no *mens rea* for the very serious charge. Mr Grubbe defended. There were three bottles - exhibits - on the table, one green, one blue, and one white. The doctor who supplied the poison as a remedy made a bit of a hash of it, although he delivered the correct warnings. Mr Crawley was suffering from an eye complaint, and Dr Lightfoot, of Watford, prescribed doses of atropine drops, mixed with a solution of rosewater. He took the green bottle, labelled POISON, to the house, personally, and told the Crawleys to be careful. On February 8th, Leonora appeared at his surgery and asked for more drops for her master. The doctor took the green bottle and said that he would refill it and bring it round later. However, he found that his supply had run out, so he went to the chemist's shop and bought a new, blue bottle of the solution, which he took to the Crawleys. Leonora was present when he issued the same warning as before, adding that the drops were even more poisonous than the previous ones, because they were fresh: 'For God's sake, be careful, and don't let the children get hold of the bottle.'

The following day, Dr Lightfoot caused confusion - a blunder, really - by turning up at the house and asking if he could have half of the contents of the blue bottle back, because another patient needed some of the atropine drops. Leonora was told to fetch another bottle, and she returned with a white one, which had held almond essence. The doctor poured half of the contents of the blue bottle into the white one, and bore away the white one, leaving the poison-labelled blue bottle. It is very feasible that this juggling about muddled the young girl.

On February 10th, there was rice pudding for dinner, cooked by Leonora. All the Crawleys were taken violently ill, in terrible agony, and the baby could have died. Mr Crawley took two to three weeks to recover. Leonora had not wanted to have any pudding, and was not ill. Three doctors were in attendance, and the police were called. There was a chorus of neighbours. Suspicion fell on the servant and the process of law began. An attempt was made to show motive. Mr Crawley said that his wife had reprimanded Leonora in the morning for not doing her job properly, but he had nothing against the girl.

In court, the Crown tried to build up an impression that she was over-proud of her cookery skills – she had made a cake for a children's picnic, and the jam tarts at Christmas – and resented being made to peel the potatoes for dinner. It was all vague, trivial and disputed. What did happen was that, feeling adventurous, and wishing to shine, she had decided to add almond essence to the pudding, stimulated, perhaps, by handling the empty white bottle which had held the flavouring. She took a bottle of it from the box on the chest of drawers upstairs. Then, she said, she realised afterwards that she had made a mistake, by putting some of the poison eye-drops in the pudding.

The County Analyst, Mr AE Elkins, stated that he found only a very small quantity of atropine in the leftover rice pudding which had been taken to him by the police. A cook would put just a little essence in a pudding, because it has a strong and over-powering taste, so this was a point in Leonora's favour. The Crown, and the judge, made much of the fact that at first, questioned by Dr Lightfoot, Leonora had denied using the blue bottle, but that would have been the first instinct of a terrified child. Later in the evening, Mr Crawley had asked her, in a kind way, what had happened, and she had confessed her mistake, but the prosecution still took its course.

Mr Justice Mathew – it was he – thought that the alleged motive was 'improbable and extraordinary' and summed up very strongly for the prisoner: 'It was a painful duty for the jury to discharge, and they would, no doubt, if they could, see a loophole, decide in her favour, but they must judge of the case as reasonable men and decide accordingly.' And so they did, returning after five minutes with a verdict of Not Guilty.

Exonerated of evil intent, Leonora returned to the real world, to her parents, John Robinson, a sanitary inspector, and Adeline (née Varney) at 172 St Albans Road, Watford, Hertfordshire. Born in January, 1883, in Liverpool, she was one of five children. The Crawleys (he was a furniture dealer), still at Queen's Road, had no domestic servant at all in 1901. Leonora disappears from sight until, an adult, she sails away from Liverpool to Canada on the 'Lake Champlain'. Roger Charles Edwin Mills, aged 22, a clerk, was on the same ship and two days after landing, the pair got married on August 12th, 1907, at York, East Toronto. They lived at 52 Bassington Avenue, York and Roger Mills worked as a brakeman. A daughter, Elsie Adeline Mills, was born on June 1st, 1908. Then, things happened, and in 1911, Elsie, without Leonora, was back in England with her grandfather, John Robinson, and his second wife, Alice. Adeline had died on February 1st, 1906. Unexpectedly, Roger Mills turns up in 1911 as a resident attendant at Horton Asylum, Epsom, Surrey. Elsie died in 1994 at Watford, and Leonora died from cerebral thrombosis on December 28th, 1966, aged 83, at St Peter's Hospital, Maldon, Essex, the widow of Roger Mills, an insurance agent.[41]

Then, as well as the fear of servants, there was the matter of Eugenics. The movement was strong at that time, well established in Europe and America by 1900. Evolving from Galton's perversion of Darwin's 'survival of the fittest', not wickedly intended, it led, of course, to total disaster in the 1930s. Many medical men, at first, were won over, and Dr Forbes Winslow was not particularly expressing a minority view, although it now reads as exaggerated and frankly wrong, when he fulminated against 'the degeneration of the human race', with a 'near proximity to a nation of madmen'. He complained that 'circumstances which ought to be controlled were causing an increase in lunacy.' He was not prepared to do anything unspeakable about compulsory sterilisation of the 'unfit', (now considered a crime against humanity) but he gladly gave advice on contracting a 'safe' marriage by observing the laws of transmission of hereditary tendency to disease of mind and body. His science was flawed, but he reflected the state of knowledge in 1899. Even Marie Stopes, a

41 It appears that Leonora dropped her string of distinctive Christian names after her ordeal and went under the more anonymous style of Miss Florence Robinson. That is the name under which she sailed to Canada, but, once there, she married with her full complement of initials – Miss Leonora AMF Robinson. It may be that she is the Florence Robinson, born in Liverpool, who was working as a kitchen maid in a substantial household, with a butler, at Scots Bridge House, Rickmansworth, Hertfordshire, in 1901. The age – 19 – is slightly wrong: Leonora would have been about 17, but could have been concealing her real age, or it could have been a common census mistake.

few years later, went beyond the benevolent bounds of Married Love and Contraception by advocating sterilisation of the 'feeble minded'. Galton and others claimed that the less intelligent were more fertile. The Ansell family in their poverty in Tankerton Street, 'tainted' (the term was used of them repeatedly in the newspapers) yet with a reproduction of ten live births, were, by contemporary thinking, just the type of carriers of bad heredity: Mary Ann, a murderer, could, in her turn, so the only partly covert reasoning went, have produced a whole dynasty of defective offspring.

SELECT BIBLIOGRAPHY

Books

Anon, *A History of Leavesden Hospital* (Hertfordshire Archives and Local Studies, Pamphlet File, Leavesden Hospital, n.d.).

Atholl, Justin, *Shadow of the Gallows* (London: John Long, 1954).

Bancroft, Margaret, *Collected Papers of Margaret Bancroft on Mental Subnormality and the Care and Training of Mentally Subnormal Children* (Philadelphia: Ware Brothers Company, 1915).

Beccle, HC, *Psychiatry: Theory and Practice for Students and Nurses* (London: Faber and Faber, 1953).

Bondeson, Jan, *Queen Victoria's Stalker: The Strange Story of the Boy Jones* (Stroud: Amberley, 2010).

Bresler, Fenton, *Reprieve: A Study of a System* (London: Harrap, 1965).

Brown, Kevin, *The Leavesden Hospital Story 1870-1995* (Horizon NHS Trust, Caterham, 1995).

Bruce, Alison, *Billington: Victorian Executioner* (Stroud: The History Press, 2009).

Connell, Nicholas and Ruth Stratton, *Hertfordshire Murders* (Stroud: The History Press, 2007).

Dawes, Frank Victor, *Not in Front of the Servants: A True Portrait of Upstairs, Downstairs Life* (London: Wayland, 1973).

Dickens's Dictionary of London, 1886.

Diplock, Monica, *The History of Leavesden Hospital* (1990).

Goodman, Jonathan, *Acts of Murder: Featuring True-Life Murder Cases Associated with Stage and Screen* (London: Harrap, 1986).

Goodman, Ruth, *How to be a Victorian* (London: Penguin, 2013).

Hollis, Matthew, *Now All Roads Lead to France: The Last Years of Edward Thomas* (London: Faber and Faber, 2011).

Horn, Pamela, *The Victorian and Edwardian Schoolchild* (Gloucester: Sutton, 1989).

Jackson, Lee, *Dirty Old London: The Victorian Fight against Filth* (New Haven: Yale University Press, 2014).

James, Mrs Eliot, *Our Servants: Their Duties to Us and Ours to Them* (London: Ward, Lock and Co., 1883).

Jones, Enid Huws, *Mrs Humphry Ward* (London: Heinemann, 1973).

McDonagh, Patrick, *Idiocy: A Cultural History* (Liverpool: Liverpool University Press, 2008).

Parry-Jones, William Ll, *The Trade in Lunacy: A Study of Private Madhouses in England in the Eighteenth and Nineteenth Centuries* (London: Routledge and Kegan Paul, 1972).

Partridge, Ralph, *Broadmoor: A History of Criminal Lunacy and its Problems* (London: Chatto and Windus, 1953).

Perkin, Joan, *Victorian Women* (London: John Murray, 1993).

Rose, Andrew, *Stinie: Murder on the Common* (London: Bodley Head, 1985).

———, *The Prince, The Princess and the Perfect Murder* (London: Coronet, 2013).

Scull, Andrew, Charlotte Mackenzie, and Nicholas Hervey, *Masters of Bedlam: The Transformation of the Mad-Doctoring Trade* (Princeton, New Jersey: Princeton University Press, 1996).

Thomas, Alison, *Portraits of Women: Gwen John and Her Forgotten Contemporaries* (Cambridge: Polity Press, 1994).

West, Donald J and Alexander Walk (eds.), *Daniel McNaughton: His Trial and the Aftermath* (Gaskell Books, 1977).

Whittington-Egan, Molly, *Doctor Forbes Winslow: Defender of the Insane* (Great Malvern: Cappella Archive, 2000).

Winslow, Dr Lyttleton Stewart Forbes, *Mad Humanity: its Forms, Apparent and Obscure* (London: CA Pearson, 1898).

———, *Recollections of Forty Years* (London: John Ousley, 1910).

———, *The Insanity of Passion and Crime* (London: John Ousley, 1912).

Wise, Sarah, *Inconvenient People: Lunacy, Liberty and the Mad-Doctors in Victorian England* (London: Bodley Head, 2012).

Short accounts of the Ansell case also appear in:

Adam, Hargrave L, *Women and Crime* (London: T. Werner Laurie, 1912).

Bailey, Brian, *Hangmen of England* (London: W.H. Allen, 1989)

Carpenter, Edward, *Prisons Police and Punishment* (Fifield, 1905)

Harrison, Paul, *Hertfordshire and Bedfordshire Murders* (Newbury: Countryside Books, 1993).

Heslop, Paul, *Hertfordshire Casebook* (Dunstable: The Book Castle, 2006).

———, *Murderous Women* (Stroud: The History Press, 2009).

Johnson, Keith, *Chilling True Tales of Old London* (Ammanford: Sigma Press, 2011).

Nash, Jay Robert, *Look for the Woman* (London: Harrap, 1984).

Pringle, Nik and Jim Treversh, *150 Years Policing in Watford District & Hertfordshire County* (Luton: Radley Shaw, 1991).

Puttick, Betty, *Hertfordshire Tales of Mystery and Murder* (Newbury: Countryside Books, 2001).

Walker, Simon, *Crime in Hertfordshire* (Dunstable: The Book Castle, 2002).

Wilson, Patrick, *Murderess* (London: Michael Joseph, 1971).

Archival collections

Contemporary Hertfordshire newspapers.

Contemporary national newspapers, especially the *Daily Mail.*

Home Office files at the National Archive ref.
  HO144/277/A61150; HO140/ 192; HO324/2+1.

Unpublished

Connell, Nicholas, *The Decline of Capital Punishment in
  Victorian Hertfordshire* (unpublished master's thesis,
  University of Cambridge, 2007).

INDEX

Index

'Mr X' (Mary Ann's fiancé), 57, 64, 68, 83–4, 87, 112
murderers: convicted female poisoners, 81–2; reprieved, 85n, 86n
Murdoch, Charles: Assistant Under-secretary at Home Office, 93; and Mary Ann's birth certificate, 82–3; correspondence from public, 93, 94, 100, 113, 125; refuses Forbes Winslow prison visit, 96; responds to petitions, 98–9, 107–8, 115; crass response to Mr and Mrs Ansell, 113; and Forbes Winslow's plea for reprieve, 131–2; back-up note on independent enquiry, 135; reacts to press criticism of Home Secretary, 137

News of the World, 46
Newton, Arthur, 159
Nicholls, Mercy, 53
Nicolson, Dr David: background, 108–9; assesses Mary Ann's mental condition, 109–12, 132; reactions to official report, 124–5, 135, 137; and Maidment case, 130
Nigeria, 160
Noakes (chandler's shop), Marchmont Street, 41, 51, 62, 63
Noakes, Emily, 41, 51
Noakes, Mrs (Croydon servant), 5

Orange, Dr William, 108
Ossulston Street, Somerstown, 163
oxalic acid, 110, 111

Pall Mall Gazette, 71, 84, 136, 148
Parish, Daniel, 25
Parish, Harriett (née Rowley; Mary Ann's cousin): false letter written in her name, 24; background, 24–5; meeting with James Ansell, 26; questioned by police, 33; evidence at inquest, 34; evidence at committal hearing, 50; possible relationship with Caroline Ansell, 99–100
Parry, Leonard A (ed.): Trial of Dr Smethurst, 73n

Passmore Edwards Settlement, Tavistock Place, 5
Pearcey, Mary Eleanor, 104
Peck, Sergeant, 34
Penfold, William F, 117
Penge Mystery (1877), 137n
Peterson, Bertha, 86n, 119
Petit Parisien, Le (newspaper), 166
petitions for mercy: appeals process, 76, 139–40; numbers, 82; City of London petition, 115–16; Daily Mail petition, 92, 101, 107–8, 126; Hemel Hempstead petition, 126; Jobson petition, 79, 115; Wisbey petition, 73, 85, 92, 96–9
Phillips, William L, 118
Phoenix Park murders (1882), 119 & n
phosphorus: bought by Mary Ann, 37, 41, 62; as cause of death in Ansell case, 32, 41–2, 50; symptoms of poisoning, 42, 60–1; lethal dose, 50; similarity between phosphorus poisoning and yellow atrophy, 49, 50, 59, 65–6, 67–8; indicated in typhoid and enteritis fevers, 60, 68; suicidal ingestion (case study), 60–1; colour of, 69–70
Pigott, PC, 35
Pope, Reverend GW, 78, 120–1, 138
Prescott, Dr (of Metropolitan Asylums Board), 120
Prescott, Charles, 118
Prince, Richard, 86n, 118, 132, 133n

Queensberry, John Douglas, 9th Marquess of, 155

railways: Hampstead Heath Station disaster (1892), 11–12; reduced fares for asylum visitors, 14
Randolph, Mr JR, 52
rat poison: bought by Mary Ann, 41, 43, 62; Mrs Molony's evidence, 38; Mr Molony's evidence, 41; Mary Ann's use of, 63; chemical analysis, 69; Mary Ann's experiments with, 70
Rawlinson, John Peel, QC: prosecutes Mary Ann, 54, 55–61, 63–5; closing

Index

www.ingramcontent.com/pod-product-compliance
Lightning Source LLC
Chambersburg PA
CBHW062213080426
42734CB00010B/1877